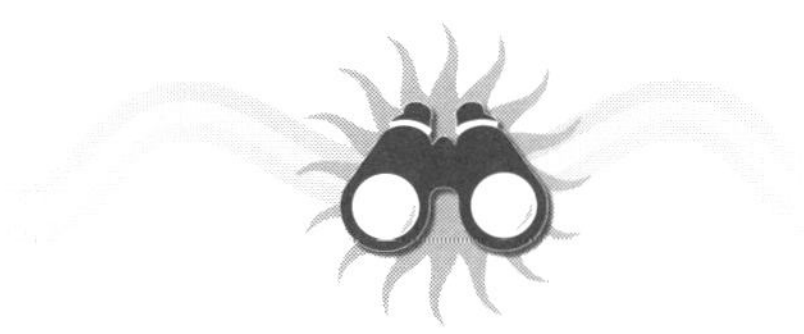

SAN JOSE Scavenger

Cassie Kifer

Copyright © 2022 by Reedy Press, LLC
Reedy Press
PO Box 5131
St. Louis, MO 63139, USA
www.reedypress.com

No part of this publication may be reproduced or transmitted in any form or by any means, electronic or mechanical, including photocopy, recording, or any information storage and retrieval system, without permission in writing from the publisher.

Permissions may be sought directly from Reedy Press at the above mailing address or via our website at www.reedypress.com.

Library of Congress Control Number: 2022937094

ISBN: 9781681064031

Cover and interior design by Claire Ford.

Cover and interior photos by the author.

Interior clipart courtesy of Pixabay and Wikimedia Commons. Galo de Barcelos clipart on page 65 courtesy Di (they-them) on Wikimedia Commons. Pastéis de Nata clipart on page 66 courtesy of K.Y.K.Z.K. on Wikimedia Commons. Serpentinite clipart on page 172 courtesy of Zimbres on Wikimedia Commons.

Printed in the United States of America
22 23 24 25 26   5 4 3 2 1

We (the publisher and the author) have done our best to provide the most accurate information available when this book was completed. However, we make no warranty, guarantee, or promise about the accuracy, completeness, or currency of the information provided, and we expressly disclaim all warranties, express or implied. Please note that attractions, company names, addresses, websites, and phone numbers are subject to change or closure, and this is outside of our control. We are not responsible for any loss, damage, injury, or inconvenience that may occur due to the use of this book. When exploring new destinations, please do your homework before you go. You are responsible for your own safety and health when using this book.

Dedication

To everyone who loves
to explore our community.

Contents

Introduction

As a traveler, I love to collect photos, trivia, and stories about the places I visit. And there's nothing I love more than sharing those discoveries with others. So, when the idea came up to build a collection of scavenger hunts featuring places in and around San Jose, I had to say yes! This sounded like a great way to expand on what I got to share in my book, *Secret San Jose: A Guide to the Weird, Wonderful, and Obscure,* and dive deeper into some other communities right in my backyard.

Though centered on San Jose, this book features 20 different neighborhoods all across Santa Clara County, stretching from Gilroy, through the East Hills up to Milpitas, over to Palo Alto, and down through the West Valley cities. Each route includes anywhere from eight to 40 sites that you can go see for yourself.

The sites I chose for these hunts draw heavily from our local history. It's something I don't think we think we share enough, and consequently, we lose more historic places and those memories every year. Along these routes you'll discover some of the oldest buildings and stories in the county, along with other places that highlight our region's diversity.

I hope that as you explore these neighborhoods you pop into local businesses, get out to explore nature, and do your own research to learn about the places featured here. I hope you will have fun as you wander these routes and gain a deeper appreciation for our community.

Please share your thoughts and your adventures with us all on social media using the hashtag #SanJoseScavenger. I can't wait to explore with you.

Legend

1 Downtown San Jose
2 Japantown
3 The Alameda
4 Willow Glen
5 East San Jose
6 Santa Clara
7 Alviso
8 Milpitas
9 East Foothills
10 Campbell
11 Los Gatos
12 Saratoga
13 Cupertino
14 Sunnyvale
15 Los Altos
16 Mountain View
17 Palo Alto
18 Stanford
19 Morgan Hill
20 Gilroy

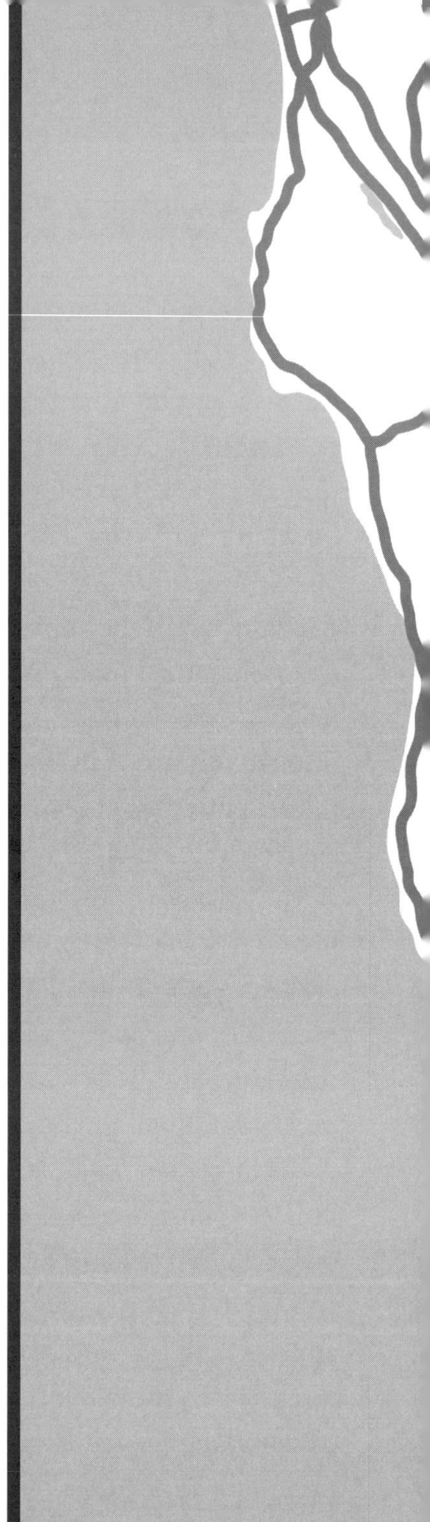

1
2
3
4
5
6
7
8
9
10
11
12
13
14
15
16
17
18
19
20

Downtown San Jose

San Jose is the 10th-largest city in the United States and the largest city in Northern California. Indigenous Tamien Ohlone people have lived in the region for thousands of years, originally in villages along the banks of the Guadalupe River. The historic downtown core of the city is the oldest developed part of Santa Clara County, around which the Pueblo of San Jose was first established in 1777. The area is a center for dining, arts, and nightlife in Silicon Valley. This hunt spans downtown to San Jose State University, and north to Julian Street.

1

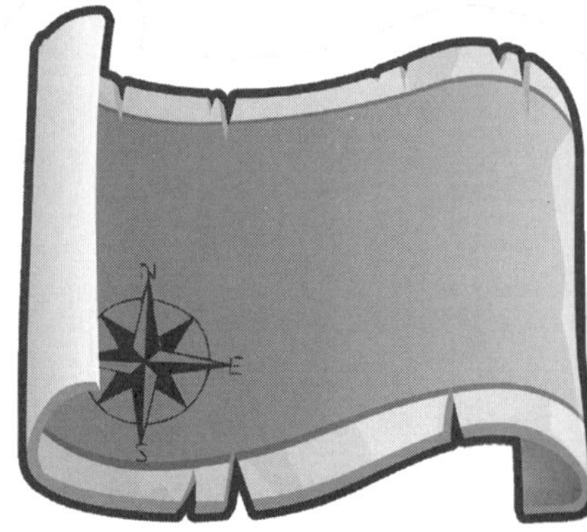

The California Dream lured them en masse;
The trek was long and dangerous, alas.
Scenes from early days and local pioneers,
A route on a map, the settlers, and steers.

2

In the tiniest park, once a parking lot,
Volunteers bring life to every new plot.
Loving veggies, inspiring kids to grow,
Sown in vibrant planters, row by row.

3

Taking your seat, you hear a ragtime tune
Rise from a piano, one of many in the room.
Looking at the keyboard, on this reprise,
There are no fingers playing these keys.

4

Once one of many that shared the same name,
Showing vaudeville acts, bawdy and tame.
Today you can watch an opera where
The neon symbolizes the name with flair.

5

This downtown haunt sat just down the road,
'Til 182 feet it was towed.
At almost five tons, this structure has proved
Among the heaviest buildings yet moved.

6

A feathered snake of indigenous lore,
Mythical figure set to rise and soar.
A grand symbol weighing over a ton,
Or, as some claim, a massive excretion?

7

The Stones, Bob Dylan, and many more
Passed through this venue when on tour.
Night after night, the crowds outside have swarmed,
Their music and art, the legends performed.

8

Once a place local families called home,
Lost in flames, forcing residents to roam.
Tragic lessons from a hate-filled past,
We mustn't return: may this history last.

9

Gathered here from across the grand new state,
The reps came to do work that would hold weight.
Often instead they implored between clinks,
"Let's have a drink, let's have a thousand drinks!"

10

First federal site the city would own,
Built from locally quarried stone.
The clocktower was lost in the Great Quake,
Today it shares creative things people make.

11

The first church in town was built on this site
Of adobe and wood, burned and rebuilt thrice.
This one, founded 1876
Was honored in name by the Roman clerics.

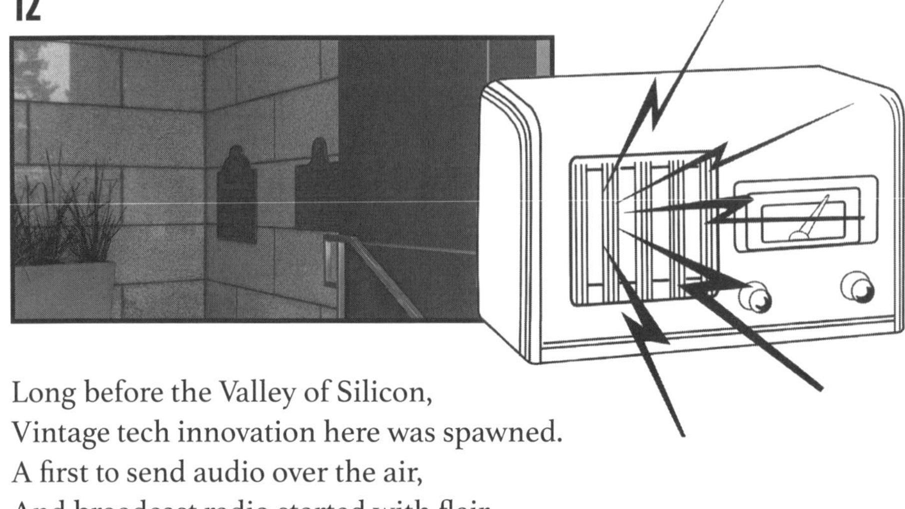

Long before the Valley of Silicon,
Vintage tech innovation here was spawned.
A first to send audio over the air,
And broadcast radio started with flair.

13

A rainbow-colored wall stands to share key
Figures who fought to change our history.
Building a city that would rise above,
Where all can be safe and love who they love.

14

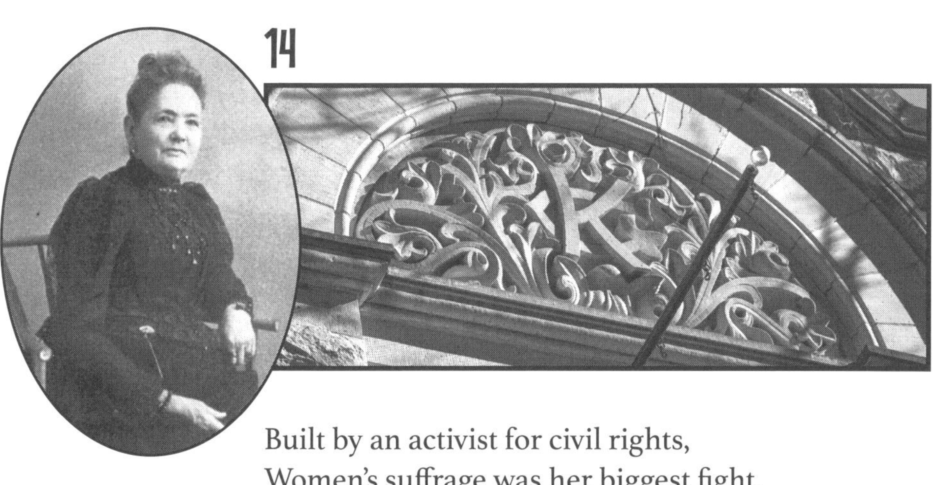

Built by an activist for civil rights,
Women's suffrage was her biggest fight.
With land from her first spouse, stone from the next,
Her woven initials are in the apex.

15

For decades this shop, loved for their passion,
Selling vintage and classic men's fashion.
The site was once a jeweler, be on the hunt,
For the name as you pass the storefront.

16

Before B of A it was B of I,
The founder Giannini was the guy.
We had the first branch outside of SF,
Later the world's largest banking outlet.

17

The oldest theater, you won't believe,
Has an odd link to Monterey Jack cheese.
Houdini performed here back in the day,
Now comedy shows are their main foray.

18

This indie cafe has a menu more lux,
And more interesting than any Starbucks.
Try the pan dulce and horchata java;
Check the foam for Selena or Frida!

19

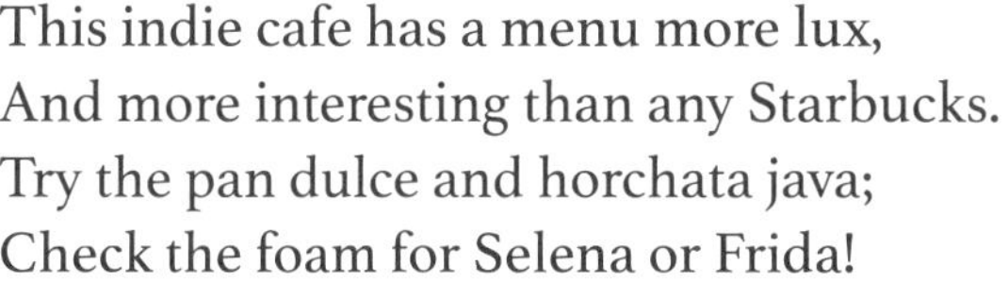

Standing against discrimination and hate,
Across the country, and here in our state.
Two students in silence on a world stage,
Honoring them and this fight we still wage.

20

Cast to honor the state's first public college,
Helping teachers to start their new voyage.
Silenced at first by the '06 Great Quake,
Still mounted down low so that it won't break.

21

Legends like Joey C. started right here,
Consuming massive portions without fear.
Can you eat it all in an hour? It's tight.
If so, win a shirt and some bragging rights.

22

A stone monolith, an ancient carved head
Far from Rapa Nui, don't be misled.
Find it at a home, south of SJ State.
Go on 5th past Bill and continue straight.

23

Once part of the old Greyhound bus station,
Named like a few others in the nation.
Sidle up to the bar at this dive spot,
Chat someone up, play the jukebox, why not?

24

Product of a noted architect's firm,
Inspired by Art Deco, you might discern.
The venue hosts performing art first-runs,
Broadway touring shows and ace productions.

25

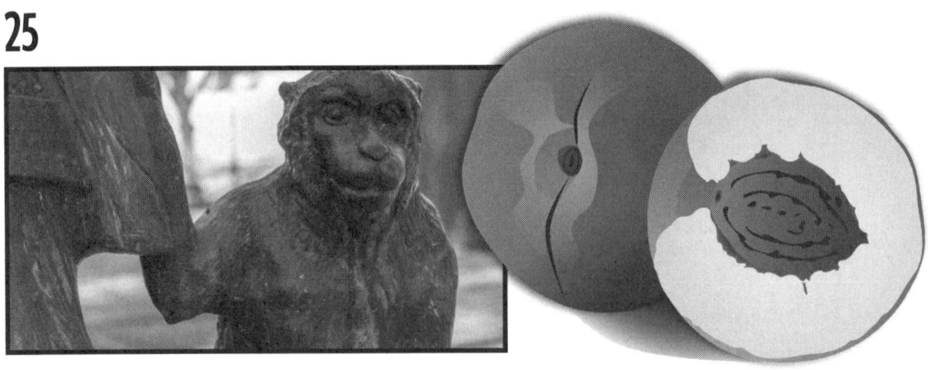

Near the river stand some statues,
Gifts from our sister on Honshu.
A boy hero named for a peach,
And three animal friends in reach.

26

Buying a home here's like nabbing Boardwalk,
But there's one spot where that's the real shock.
It's a place where you can say, without fail,
Do not pass go, go directly to jail.

27

Asked the Pope to protect her family,
One clear, inspiring act of bravery.
Lotus in one hand, globe in another,
Stating all kids deserve a better future.

28

Rivers, the source of civilization,
Life flows from nature in every nation.
Wild things share this land as home or passage.
Find this vibrant mural spanning a bridge.

29

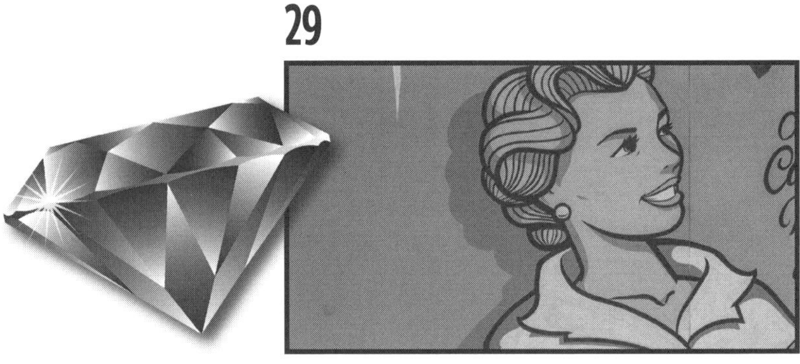

A family-run shop over the years,
No doubt removing the greasiest of smears.
Recently restored, this promo mainstay,
The oldest billboard in all the South Bay.

30

Testament to abundant life and grace,
Reasons to delight in this lovely space.
Recalling a valley once based in ag,
Annual harvests were reason to brag.

31

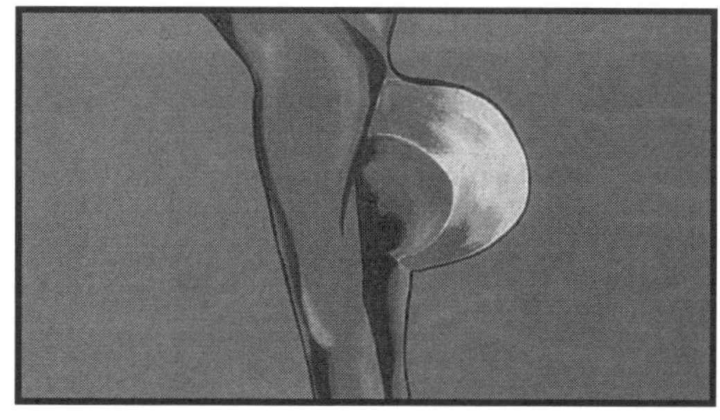

The Diving Diva adorns this side wall,
A landmark venue where travelers call.
Promoting their once famous outdoor pool
That's only a memory now, how cruel.

The place to go when visitors are near,
Even picky eaters can find something here.
A sign recognizable in the dark,
Modeled on that of a Seattle landmark.

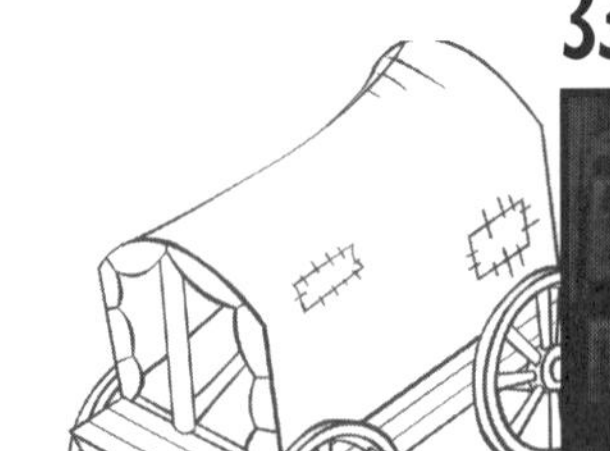

33

The oldest home in all of San Jose,
In a nightlife destination's walkway.
Recently credited to the builder,
Adding his surname to the nomenclature.

34

Can you spot our longest-occupied church?
Carved wood from the steeple down to the earth.
Redwood detail was crafted by one man,
A shipbuilder and retired sea captain.

35

Built here as part of a clever crusade,
To lure the capital back, it failed, I'm afraid.
Did you know that in the basement dwells
A dungeon and long-forgotten jail cells?

36

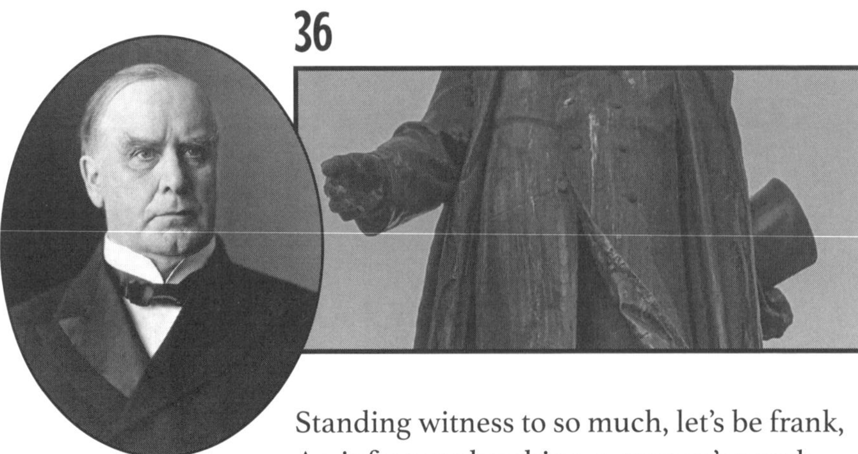

Standing witness to so much, let's be frank,
An infamous lynching, a cannon's prank.
He lost this weapon in a time of protest,
Now he stands alone, still nattily dressed.

37

An image in bronze of a guy who would
Go on to name a downtown neighborhood.
Union General in the Civil War,
Later a brandy-distilling czar.

38

Along the wall bronze placards hang,
Plain words, but they hit with a bang.
Spoken by those who risk their life
To save us from fire, crashes, or strife.

39

Stop in for curry or a pint of ale,
Chat up a neighbor to tell you a tale.
The building was a grocery, brothel, then jail.
Oft said to be haunted, the ghost might bewail.

Japantown

This vibrant San Jose neighborhood is one of the last three historic Japantown communities in the United States. This neighborhood, adjacent to the historic Heinlenville Chinatown, was established by Japanese and later Filipino immigrants as they settled in the Santa Clara Valley. This hunt covers Japantown and neighboring Ryland and Northside communities.

1

Art inspired by a famous woodblock print,
It's a new design on an old imprint.
Adorning a much-loved family store,
Strawberry mochi, pickles, poke, and more.

2

Retro pink sign watching over the street,
a place for the community to meet.
This building and local institution,
was built by members of the congregation.

3

Once the local office of Hop Sing Tong,
Branch of a group once nationally known.
For mutual aid and brotherhood,
Helping each other when no one else would.

4

Many cultures have called this block home,
Black, Chinese, and Japanese all have come.
But this address is a gathering place,
"Pinoytown," as locals now call this space.

5

The oldest building in Japantown stood,
When the street, then called Heinlenville, would
Serve as a boarding house, later restaurant,
Dishing out chop suey at this much-loved haunt.

6

Oldest restaurant in the neighborhood,
Loved by all for their homestyle food.
Giving a gift to kids who come to eat,
Tickets to redeem for toys or a treat.

7

Once the community's first theater,
Kabuki, vaudeville, movies, and more.
Fading over the years as TV grew in haste,
Today it's a church for an Ethiopian faith.

8

Soft, pillowy bites of glutinous rice,
The colors and textures will entice.
For seven decades, this local shop
Has rolled them by hand on their tabletop.

9

Once a famed Chinese restaurant in town,
Owner Bill Dair was of local renown.
Entertaining all of San Jose's elite:
Only the neon remains of this retreat.

Modeled after one in Kyoto city,
Built by local brothers in the thirties.
With side-gabled roof and hand-carved wood,
The heart and center of the neighborhood.

11

A winding granite form helps all to see,
A timeline of local history.
And sharing values the first-gen Issei,
Gave to the second that they called Nisei.

12

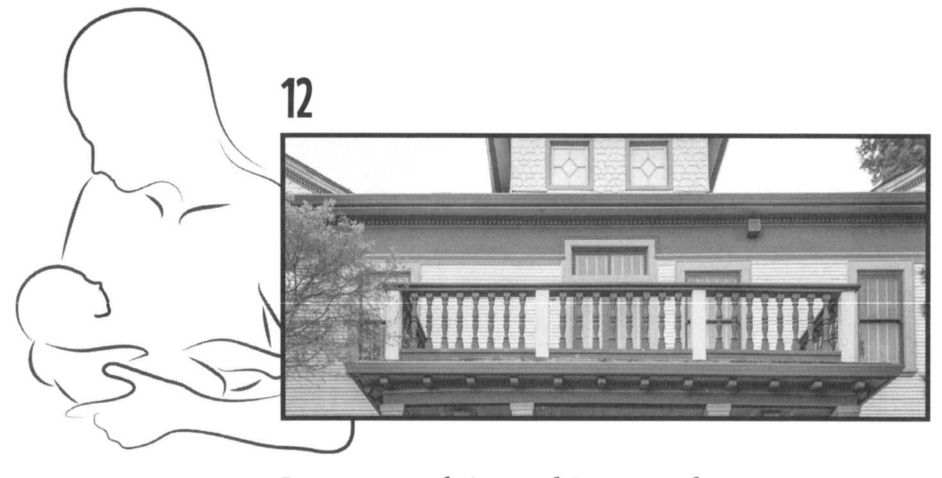

In segregated times, this was a place
Where Japanese folks were treated with grace,
Where babies were born and essential care
Was given to all for local welfare.

13

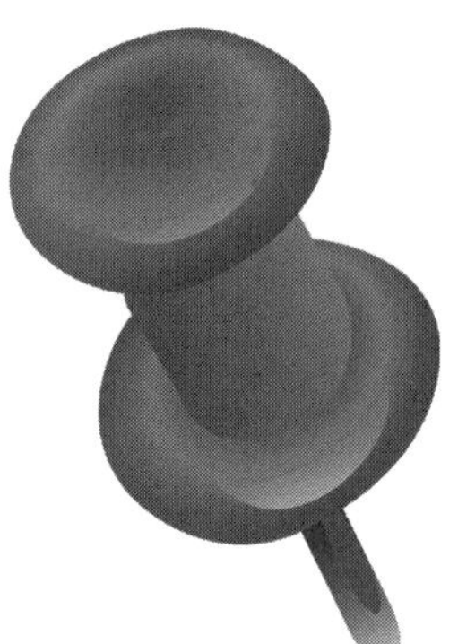

ANCESTRY

Living in the Following Area:

he County of Santa Clara, State of California, lying generally north and north
t the point on the Santa Cruz-Santa Clara County line, due west of a line draw
ue east along said line through said peak to its intersection with Llagas Creek
Madrone to the point where it is crossed by Llagas Avenue; thence northeaste
01; thence northerly on said Highway No. 101 to Cochran Road; thence northeast
eley Road; thence easterly on Steeley Road to Madrone Springs; thence along a
to its intersection with the Santa Clara-Stanislaus County line; together with
ously covered by Exclusion Orders of this Headquarters.

Pinned up on a pole for all to see,
A moving reminder of dark history.
Exact words that our government once used,
Imprisoning our neighbors, wrongly accused.

14

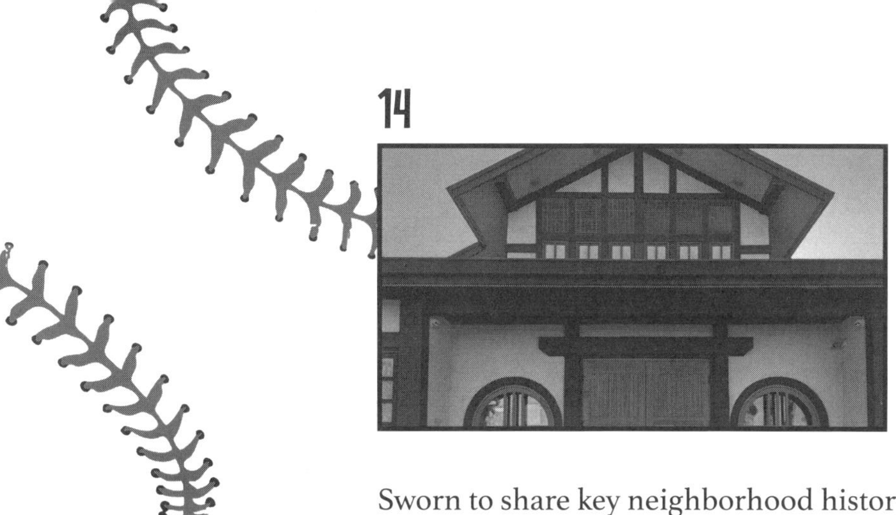

Sworn to share key neighborhood history,
Through Japanese American families.
Agriculture, baseball, and more
And a dark legacy of the last World War.

15

Japanese art and vibrant textiles,
Kimono and yukata, in many styles.
You can't miss the mural outside that shows
A blue dog . . . or wolf? Or dragon? Who knows?

16

A place of respite from the summer heat,
This venue's cooling power couldn't be beat.
Vintage Batchelder tiles were a grand slam,
Set in a city, maybe Amsterdam?

17

Painted on a home, some local insight,
A famous place that was once on this site.
The grandest hotel in all of the town,
But sadly, the Great Quake brought it down.

18

The Pueblo of San Jose was founded here,
As the Guadalupe River was so near.
But because every rain flooded the town,
They up and moved it almost two miles down.

19

All are welcome despite ability,
A unique place built by the Rotary.
Colorful, hands-on toys all around,
Native plant and wildlife themes abound.

20

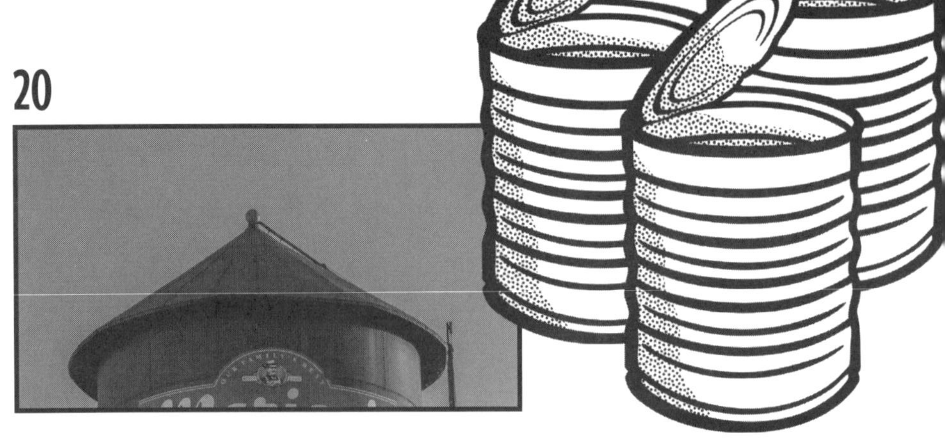

On this block once was one of many
Fruit packing houses and a cannery.
The high-reaching sign with Italian brand,
One lasting reminder of that time span.

21

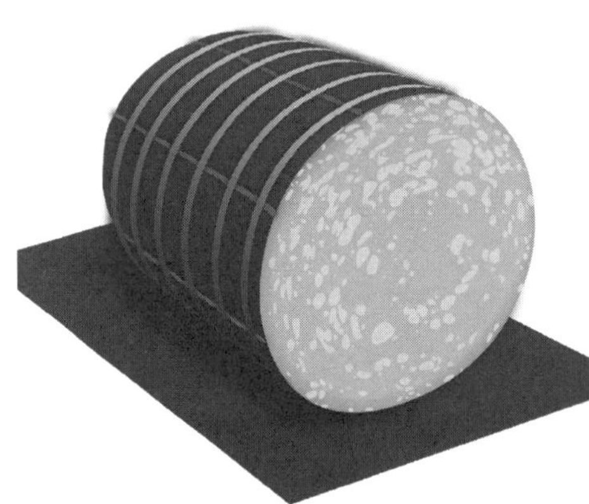

This little shop has served eaters
For well over a hundred years.
Stop by for lunch to grab a bite.
The sausages are always right.

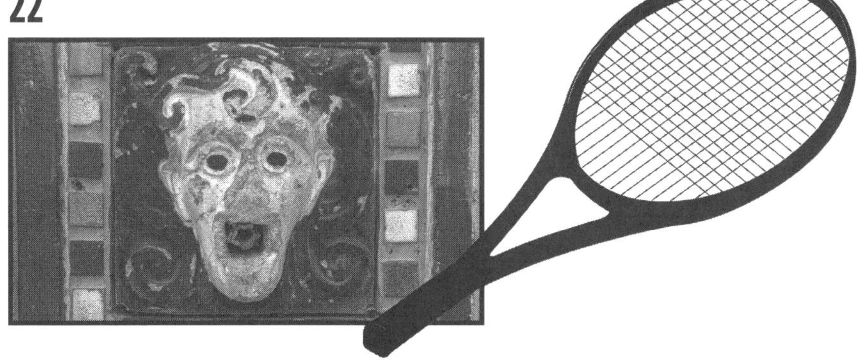

Colorful ceramic tiles adorn
A fountain that will soon be restored.
A doctor's tribute, the park's namesake,
Folks play tennis, volleyball, and bocce 'til late.

23

Stop in to visit these homeless pets,
You surely will not have any regrets.
Just beware, I bet you will be smitten,
And want to take home a cat or a kitten.

24

Home to a key show for one famous band,
Though on another address it now stands.
They lined up down the street, hundreds of guests,
One of the first so-called "Acid Tests."

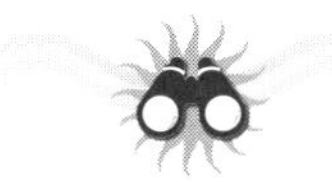

The Alameda

The Alameda was first built more than 200 years ago as a transportation and commerce route connecting the Pueblo of San Jose to Mission Santa Clara. This hunt covers The Alameda and around, from just west of Downtown San Jose through the Rose Garden neighborhood.

1

Peek-a-boo! Watch out for the kids who hide
In these works of art, along the path's side,
On the paved trail at an urban park,
Near the arch at Little Italy's start.

2

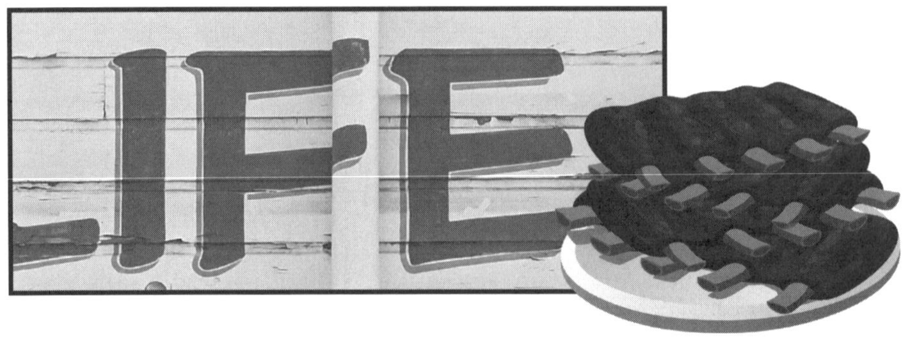

Founded as a hotel and lodging site,
Workers from Italy stayed overnight.
This classic bar and grill is loved by fans
Last stop before the arena stands.

3

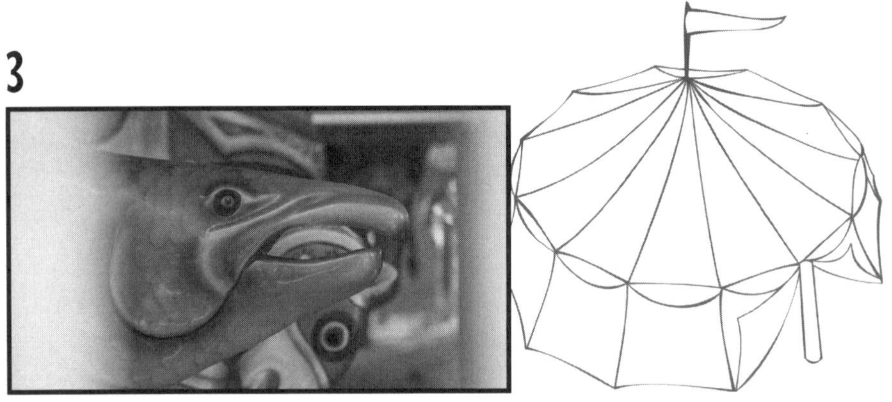

Open just a few years before it stopped,
Spinning around under the Big Top.
A shark and camel are cast in this show,
Will it run again? I hope, but who knows?

4

This downtown venue has held many names,
Various laptops, now enterprise frames.
A venue that's commonly called The Tank,
Too cold for the mascot to live, to be frank.

5

This neighborhood park, if I am correct,
Named for an early San Jose architect.
All around the play structure made for kids
Hang labels from locally packed fruit lids.

6

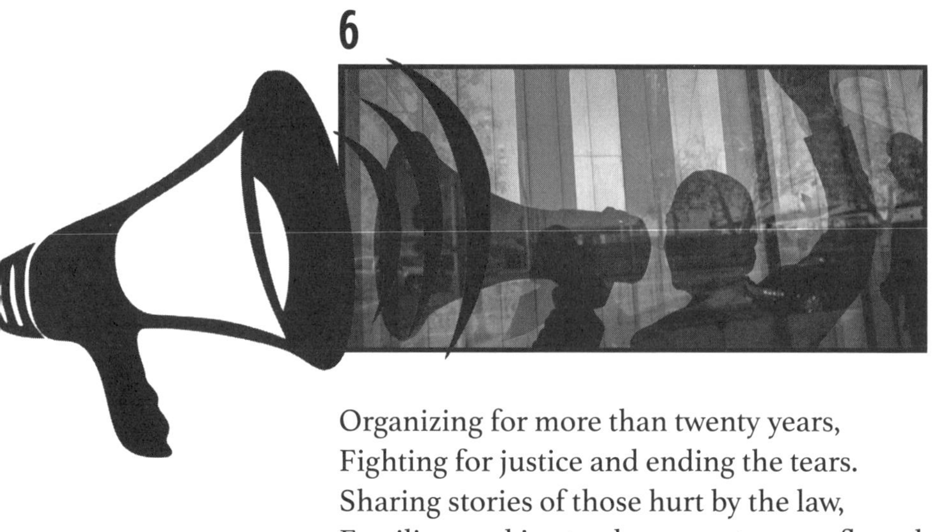

Organizing for more than twenty years,
Fighting for justice and ending the tears.
Sharing stories of those hurt by the law,
Families working to change systems so flawed.

7

A bakery near the train tracks may
Serve up unique treats made fresh each day.
Plush bags of bread, still warm from the oven,
And sticky baklava: there's so much I'm lovin'!

8

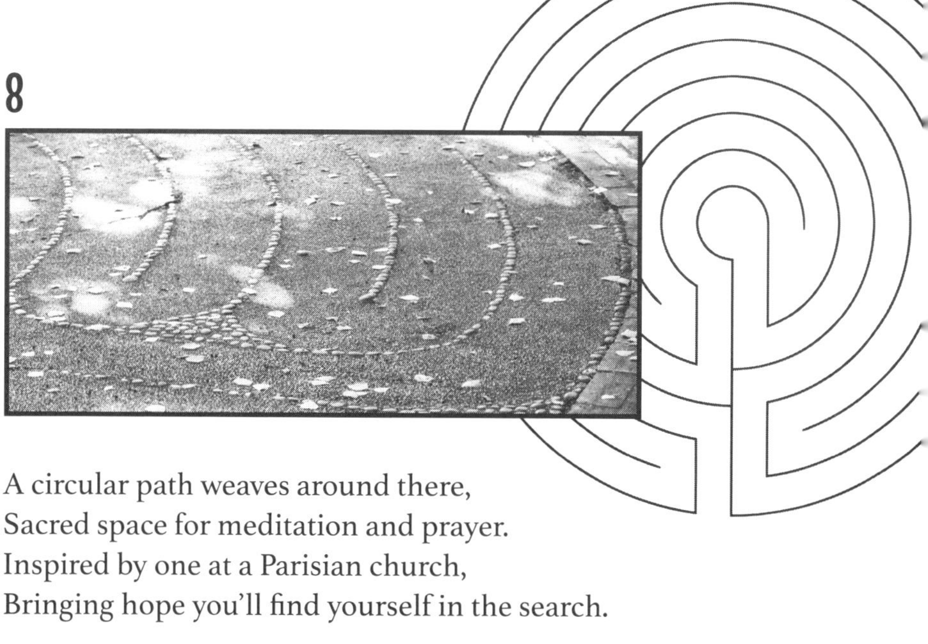

A circular path weaves around there,
Sacred space for meditation and prayer.
Inspired by one at a Parisian church,
Bringing hope you'll find yourself in the search.

9

There once was a large mansion on this site,
Home to a clan, ever in the spotlight.
Owners of a popular downtown store,
Victims of a crime, stuff of local lore.

10

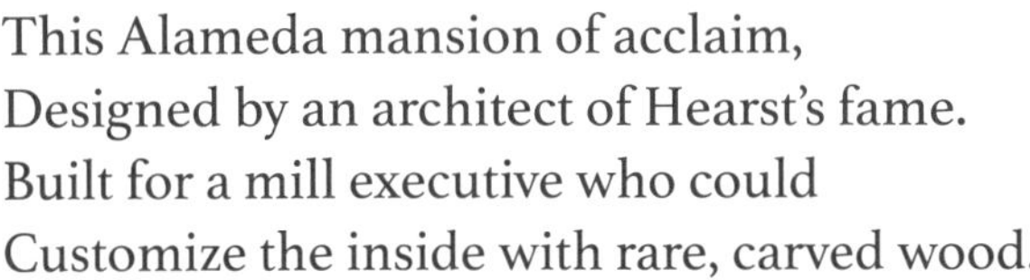

This Alameda mansion of acclaim,
Designed by an architect of Hearst's fame.
Built for a mill executive who could
Customize the inside with rare, carved wood.

11

Old brick arches still standing mark the way,
To a so-called park, but not a place to play.
Developed back in 1893,
Watch for these markers on Singletary.

12

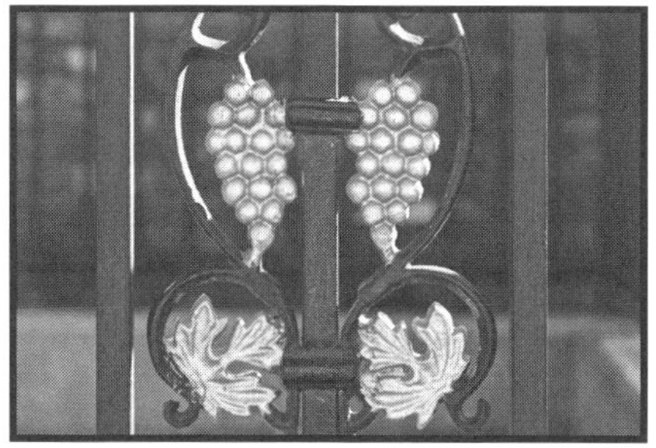

On this site, more than a century combined,
They've been fermenting stuff: first beer, now wine.
It once looked like a castle or mansion,
The brick facade survived demolition.

13

Steel-covered walls and a cherubic frieze,
Enter inside and be transported, please.
Imagine a Balinese jungle so lush,
Asian designs and zen space give you a rush.

14

This mural up on the corner has proved
Iconic, though the shop has long since moved.
A nonprofit known for this vivid macaw,
Rescuing pets that fly, slither, or have paws.

15

This store might look small, but venture inside,
Labyrinthine maze, quiet places to hide.
And watch out for their famous furry staff,
Who, on any day, might hide or make you laugh.

16

This ornate building, once a car showroom,
Built in the ’20s, the early auto boom.
Today these wide-open floor plan rooms are
Space for engineers and designers, not cars.

17

At a shop named for the nearby station,
Beneath neon signs at the window’s junction.
Depicting a scene of childhood’s small joys,
Watch out for these mischievous little boys.

18

This old loading dock surrounded by homes,
Through it the Valley's rich harvest would flow.
Named for a loved stone fruit and a sweet treat,
These drivers would ship it out via their fleet.

19

Since the '60s, holding fort here,
Like a few others, far and near.
Looking down from twenty two feet,
The tallest guy you'll ever meet.

20

This retro neon sign hangs right near downtown,
Shimmies past dark for all who come 'round.
Former site of a sausage factory,
This dancing figure will fill you with glee.

21

On the spot where the cannery once stood,
People came 'round whenever they could
To enjoy the playground, play some footy,
To let their dogs run, or just play hooky.

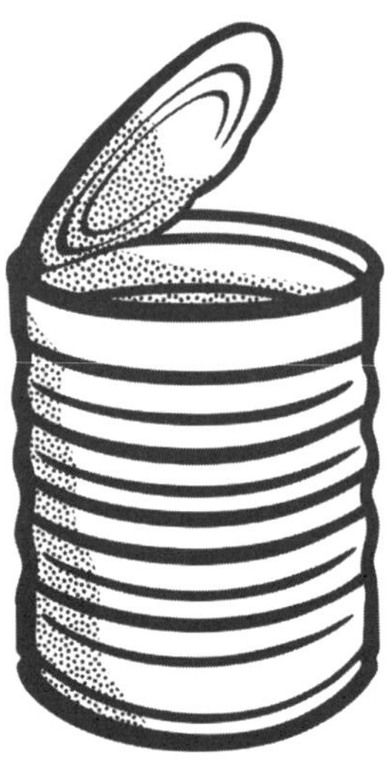

22

Right here where this community now stands,
Workers packed fruit for a famed canning brand.
It's been said that these frugal workers had
Invented the humble mixed fruit salad.

23

Demo space for a design laboratory,
Offering ideas, things you can see.
Learning about our native landscapes,
Greening our yards, and changes to make.

24

Columns across the building's entrance span
Spiritual home of a secretive clan.
Where they host their meditation efforts,
Healing sessions for the sick and the hurt.

25

Designed by the famous architect Weeks,
Since the '30s, inspiring delighted shrieks.
This historic room for shows long and short,
At first built to be a place to play sports.

26

Once a prune orchard, now a place to stroll,
Famous for flora from spring through the fall.
Large collection of fragrant blooms attest,
A garden some have called America's best.

____

____

27

Driving down Bascom, see the colonel's note,
"Finger lickin' good!" is what he wrote.
One of only two last buckets to see,
And the oldest-standing in the country.

____

____

Willow Glen

In the late 1800s, this neighborhood southwest of Downtown San Jose was known as the "Willows" and was made up of a number of small farms. Later a small business district grew up, centered on Lincoln Avenue. Willow Glen was incorporated into San Jose in 1936. This hunt stretches from the southern part of the community, through the downtown business district, and into North Willow Glen.

1

While picket fences aren't a frequent sight,
This suburban tract still has them in spite.
Watch out for the white entry gates that share
The neighborhood's initials: "W" and "R."

2

Watch as you walk through these historic tracts,
And try to spot these aging sidewalk stamps.
Sharing the famed mid-century builder,
This one's on Fairwood, across from a corner.

3

This Victorian home has been faithfully fixed
Since it was damaged in the Great Quake of '06.
The owners nearly killed by falling bricks,
They ripped out the fireplaces to cut further risk.

4

Built for a family that had to be tough,
With an odd name: Great? No, just good enough.
Recently named as a city landmark,
They're working to restore it, part by part.

5

When driving toward downtown Willow Glen,
Spot this quirky street sign at a junction,
Near a house whose family in another time
Was killed in an infamous Campbell crime.

6

Find an unexpected storefront,
When on this residential street you jaunt.
They once sold gifts and before that fixed clocks,
An offbeat sight, if you ever here walk.

7

A mod relief on this churchfront tower,
Going nearly all the way up the spire.
On a street named for seasonal stone fruit,
A unique pattern, that you can't refute.

8

Walking your dog on the main drag,
And now it's time for lunch to snag.
Park your well-behaved pooch here,
Pick small, medium, or large gear.

9

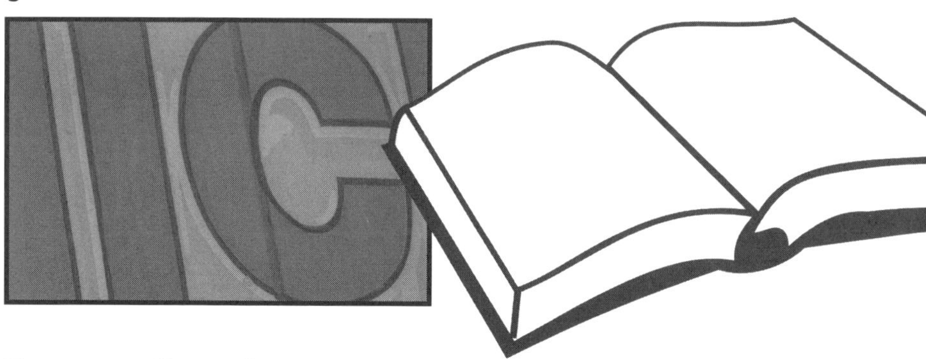

For now, well over forty years,
Folks young and old have been stopping here
To check out the best seller list,
Or grab something new that they might have missed.

10

Neon blooms on a glowing marquee,
Lighting the street for all to see.
While you can't watch a movie now,
You can send a letter somehow.

11

A member of the Tamien community,
Built his home here in the 1830s.
One of the last remaining of its kind,
Newer in front, and the adobe behind.

12

California dreaming when I see
Streets marked by such a stunning canopy.
This group right here has been said to be
Designated as our "heritage trees."

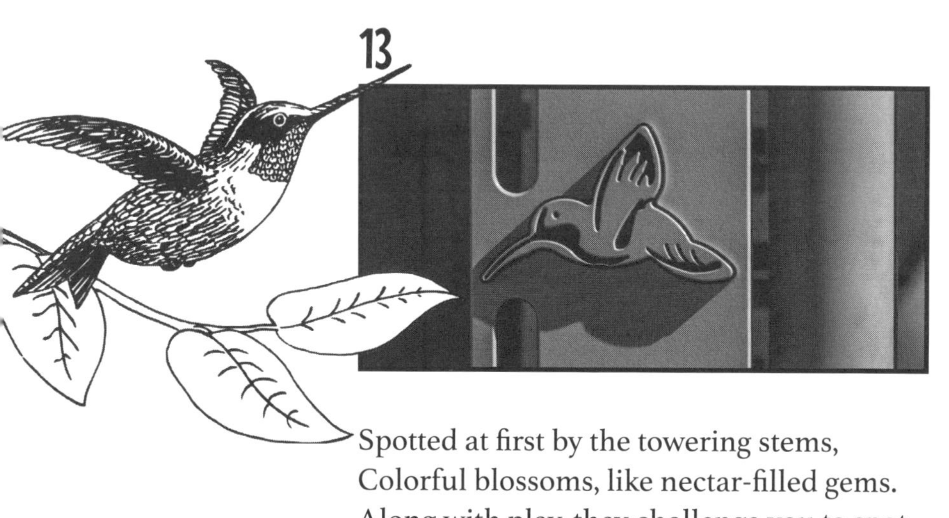

13

Spotted at first by the towering stems,
Colorful blossoms, like nectar-filled gems.
Along with play, they challenge you to spot
Pollinators flitting around the plot.

14

San Jose's first home in the famed Prairie style
Was built for the designer all the while.
The city's most prolific architect
Knew this was a style we'd want to protect.

15

Built for the Flemings, this Victorian cottage,
They lived there with John Holmes, son by marriage.
Holmes is well-known in local history,
Famously hung by a mob in '33.

16

A much-loved mural on the handball court,
A timeless symbol that brings comfort.
Painted by an artist from the neighborhood,
Later restored from the elements it withstood.

East San Jose

This region, also known as the East Side or East Valley, spans some of San Jose's most diverse neighborhoods and is a cultural center and home to large Latino, Portuguese, Vietnamese, and other communities. East San Jose was once a separate city that was annexed by San Jose in 1911. This hunt starts just east of downtown, through the Naglee Park and Roosevelt neighborhoods around Santa Clara Street, continuing on Alum Rock Avenue and south to Tully Road.

1

It hides the fact, this quaint brick backdrop,
That you are dining in an old auto shop.
This local favorite was once aptly
Featured on a show by Guy Fieri.

2

Mystery figures, heads, and limbs,
With cryptic phrases, this yard brims.
The work of artist Ted Fullwood,
Find it in the Naglee neighborhood.

3

"Listen to the music" of this neighborhood,
And spot the home where a famed band once lived.
Not "what a fool believes," it is clear,
Some of their top tunes were written here.

4

The Naglee Park neighborhood's first home base
Once belonged to the land's namesake.
This mansion where the general would reside,
Now with a mix of apartments inside.

5

This bashful face in a tint of green
Looks like an artichoke or cabbage, it seems.
Find it in a wall on 17th,
Near where a major street crosses the creek.

6

Post-Civil War San Jose's population boomed;
Many Black families from the South here moved.
Founded in 1864 to be
The first to serve this growing community.

7

This is one great place for locals to come,
Especially those seeking tastes of home.
South and Central America are their forte,
With hard-to-find foods from each Latin country.

8

This little house on Santa Clara Street,
Back in the generation of the Beats.
Once home of Neal Cassady and his pack,
Crash pad for friends like Ginsberg and Kerouac.

9

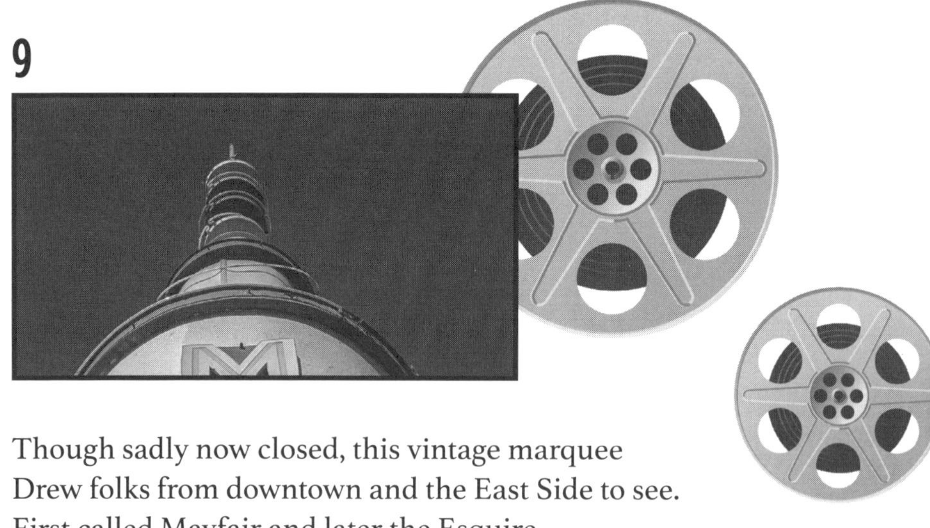

Though sadly now closed, this vintage marquee
Drew folks from downtown and the East Side to see.
First called Mayfair and later the Esquire,
With this unique, cylindrical tower.

10

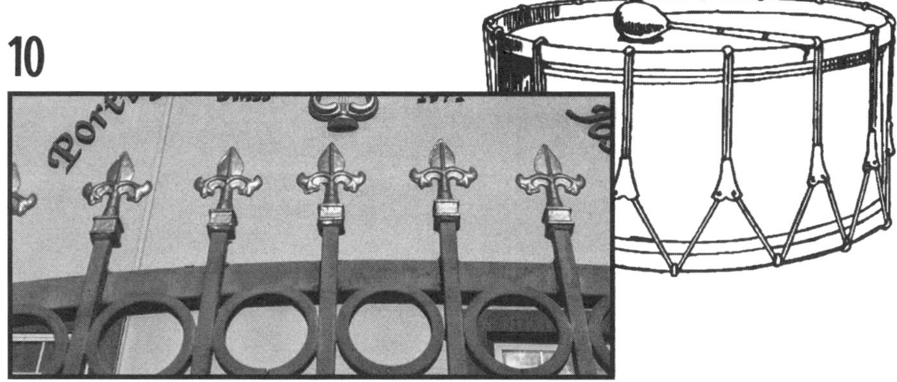

The sound of the horn and drums will tease,
"Banda Velha," "Old Band" in Portuguese.
This performing group will often play
At local events and on holidays.

11

These resources have served families here
For more than a hundred years.
Funded by a wealthy East Coaster, you see,
Last one near here that's still a library.

12

From the World Fair's Portugal display they gleaned
Things to build this place in 1915.
A scenic cultural institution,
A place of faith and the city's evolution.

____

____

13

This tiny east side corner store
Is the size of a closet and no more.
Where Island folks come for staple foods,
Polynesian, mostly, and the Caribbean, too.

____

____

14

The largest of the kind across the Bay,
A market and restaurant spanning a walkway.
Selling regional food, wine, and liquor
From Portugal, Azores, Brazil, and more.

15

The first-ever restaurant in San Jose,
Prestigiously ranked by a tire company.
The only Portuguese spot with this cert,
Known for seafood and elegant desserts.

16

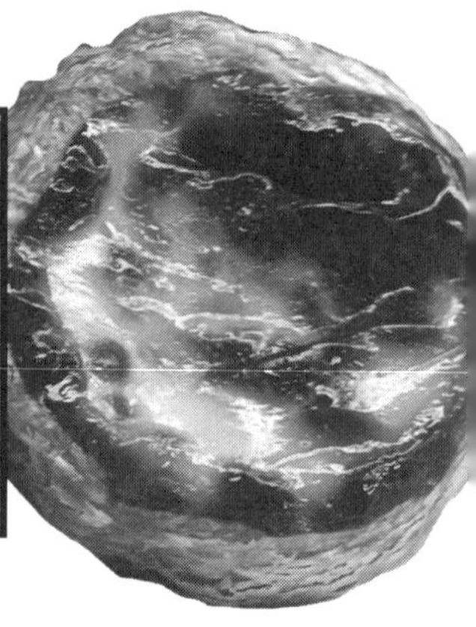

Crafting sweet round tarts with a lovely sheen,
In flavors of almond, orange, or bean.
Pastries that everyone adores,
Plus breads typical of the Azores.

17

Local legends: do you know them? If not,
They're one of San Jose's most famous bands.
Once the site of a farmworker boycott
Where this community center now stands.

18

Nostalgic sight for local families,
Getting hungry when this sign is seen.
A place to stop for colorful pan dulce,
Sweets, pastries, and treats to load on your tray.

19

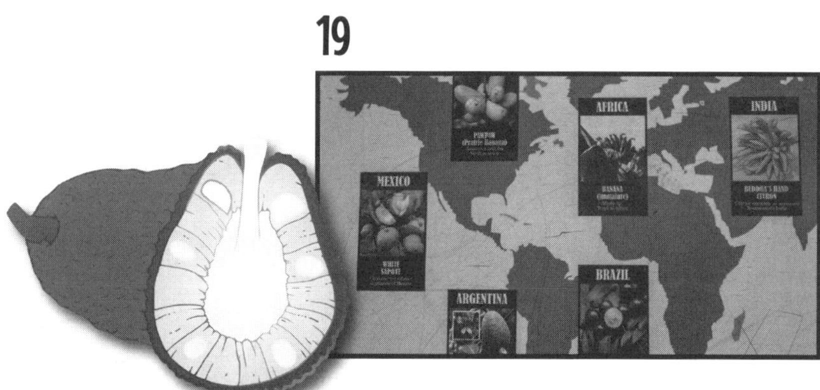

Travel the world through this orchard of fruit,
Colorful and ripe, these are a beaut.
With more than one hundred varieties,
And some you've never heard of, certainly.

20

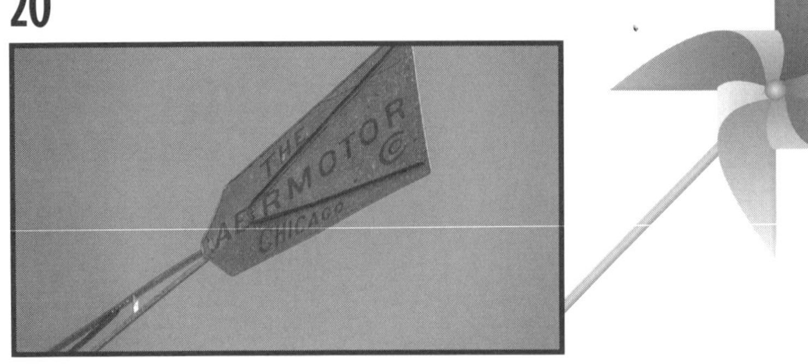

Built to draw water from storage so deep
Below the surface, more than 400 feet.
Once this piece of vintage technology
Powered farms as far as the eye could see.

21

You might be surprised to find this place here,
Descending the off-ramp, it will appear.
Fields of green among this urban span,
Growing food for a Saturday farm stand.

22

Find this site at a key intersection,
For car clubs, activists, and celebration.
This building hides dozens of places to stop,
Small businesses, and mom-and-pop shops.

23

Drive through this neighborhood near Story Road,
And find place names from a fairy-tale world.
Cinderella, Peter Pan, are roads to follow,
Also Van Winkle, Cotton Tail, and Sleepy Hollow.

24

Honoring this, the opuntia cactus,
a staple common in local practice.
Planted here by the community,
With other foods that nourish families.

25

Fragments of glass sharing long history,
From Ohlone culture to worker unity.
Where once a leader was recruited then shaped,
Fighting for his ignored neighborhood's sake.

26

Once the home of a civil rights leader,
He learned to build power and became a great speaker.
Talking to neighbors, going door to door,
Skills that built a union of farm workers.

27

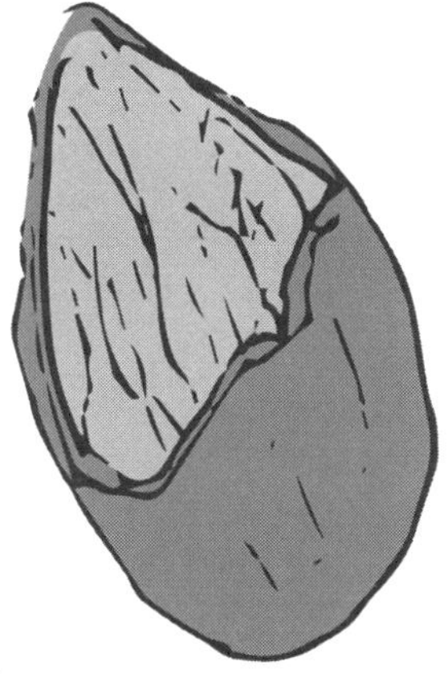

Heading towards the hills, watch for the line
Stretching down the street at opening time.
Since the '30s, a family-owned spot,
Known for burnt almond and treats highly sought.

28

This curious building and roadside kitsch,
Built to sell orange juice, what a switch.
Drawing guests to the east side from near and far,
This venue brings hot dogs and floats to your car.

29

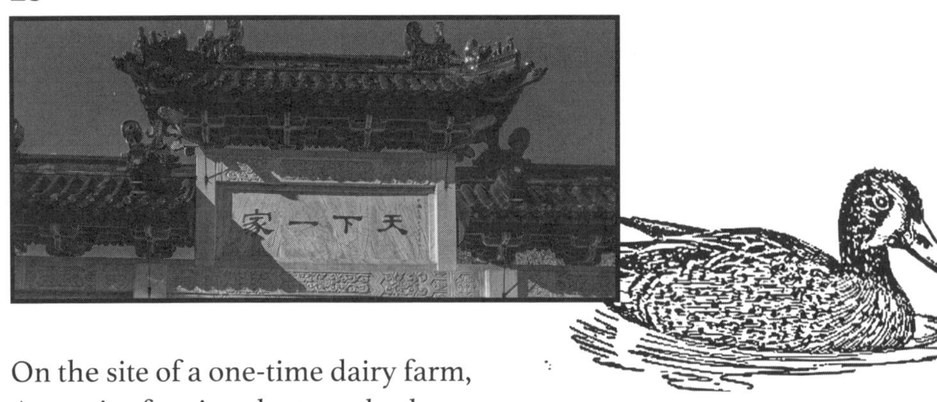

On the site of a one-time dairy farm,
An oasis of native plants and calm.
To honor historic leaders and people,
Architecture and pagoda steeples.

30

A popular spot for coffee, lunch, or
Meeting under this dramatic figure.
Famed military leader of Vietnam,
Defeating Mongol forces and Kublai Khan.

31

Hidden behind a big-box store lot,
Catch a glimpse of this one on the next plot.
Guiding you to a temple and garden,
Where dozens of Buddha statues stun.

32

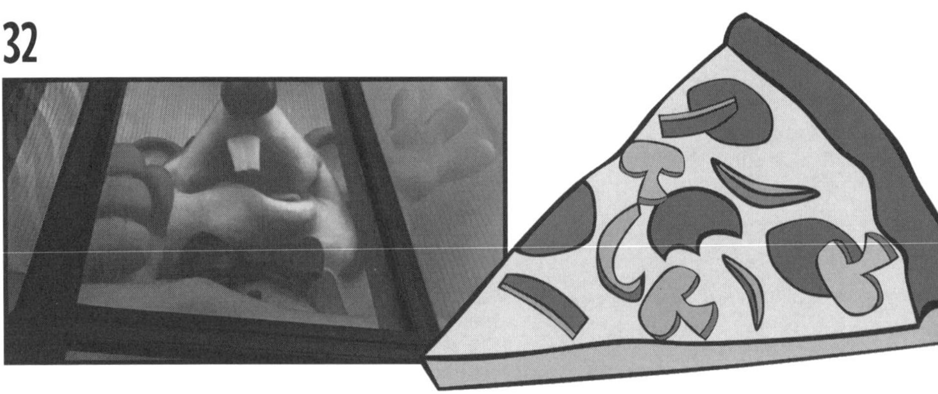

Where can one find as rare a monument
To our town as this thirty-foot rodent?
In the alcove of a former toy store,
Now palace to kids' entertainment and more.

Santa Clara

In 1977, Franciscan padres founded the eighth California mission, Mission Santa Clara, in the valley along the Guadalupe River. Today, Santa Clara (nicknamed "the Mission City"), is home to many corporate and tech headquarters, diverse neighborhoods, and Santa Clara University. This hunt spans the mostly residential areas of Santa Clara, south of Highway 101.

1

Tucked into a quiet neighborhood,
This place has a record that has withstood.
Over fifty Olympic medals won over the years,
And 23 world records have been set right here.

2

For generations, this mom-and-pop shop
Lured folks from across the Bay to stop.
For a sweet treat with some serious clout,
Don't wake up late, they sell out!

____

____

3

Where the first chartered college in the state once stood,
If you blink you'll miss it, watch if you could.
Today you'll find it at the corner of the road,
At a parking lot where police cars are stowed.

____

____

4

Founded by padres at the mission church,
To honor loved ones who have left this earth.
Eternal tributes for all to see,
Including the famous Tiburcio V.

5

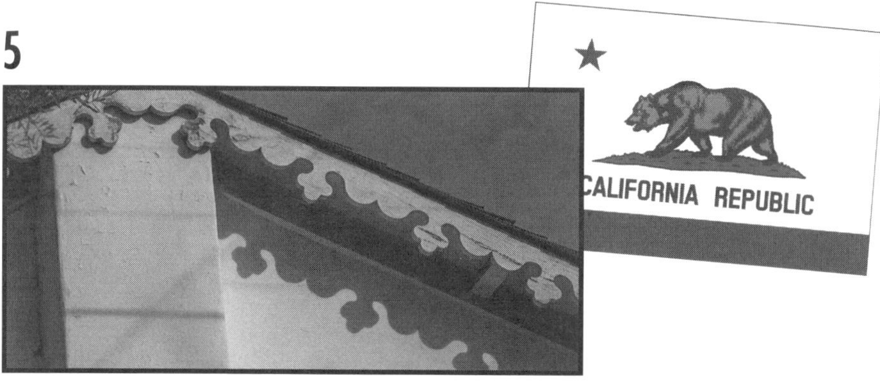

The oldest home in town has a tall tale;
It may have also been a mission jail.
First owned by a settler named Galindo,
Another died in the Bear Flag imbroglio.

6

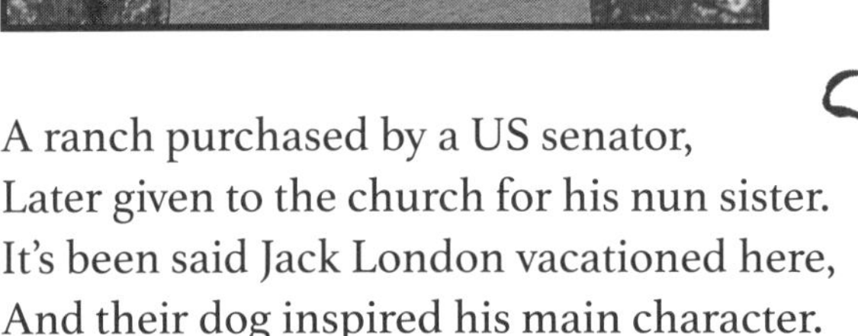

A ranch purchased by a US senator,
Later given to the church for his nun sister.
It's been said Jack London vacationed here,
And their dog inspired his main character.

____

____

7

Marking the one Mexican War battle
That happened right here in Northern Cal.
This angular park and pergola were
Named for a three-decade city planner.

____

____

8

This crucial creative address displays
Work by artists from all across the Bay.
Exhibits that share local history,
Others, found back here, more contemporary.

9

This house has a markedly famous porch,
Moved piece by piece from Hiram Bond's old ranch.
Noted because a local myth arose,
London wrote *Call of the Wild* here, as it goes.

10

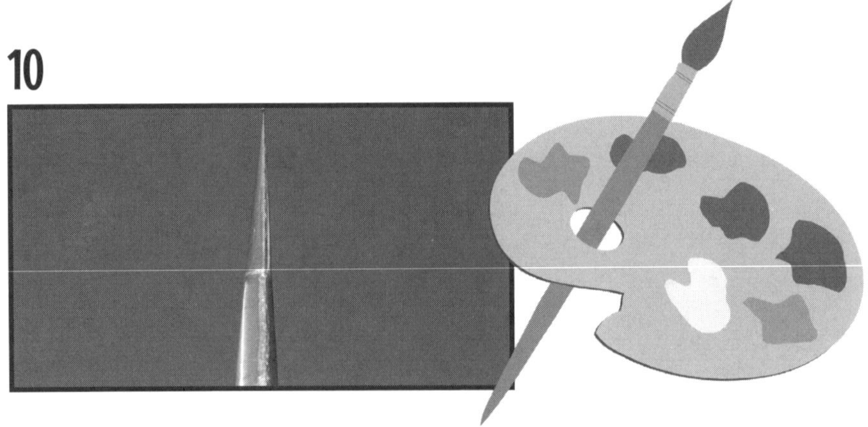

Though resembling a weapon of war,
It serves a kind goal, though looks bizarre.
Designed by an Italian avant-garde
Who advocated for free public art.

____

____

11

Stroll into the past with this tour on foot:
From first people until now, they've put
All this history on 20-plus plaques
You can find at city hall, near the back.

____

____

12

Built as home for a medical doctor,
The first to work in the town, as it were.
Where's the front door? There are two, you can see,
One for his office, one the pharmacy.

13

A fine example of the Queen Anne style,
An ornate mansion that could beguile.
First owned by a seed company founder,
Now SCU sorority girls live here.

14

The historic downtown met a sad fate,
Like many other suburban towns of late.
Torn down to pursue redevelopment,
Find these images nearby to get a sense.

15

The oldest structures on the whole site,
This one lone wall and building to the right.
The historic church was ruined by fire,
So they built the one that today we admire.

16

A scientific space named for a priest,
Known to forecast the weather and heat.
For this he earned a suitable nickname,
(We need him today!) "Padre of the Rains."

17

Built by a carpenter, as you can see,
The fine wood detailing at the roof's peak.
One of a few homes, this Italian Gothic,
That survived the quake in 1906.

18

This domicile under the pines,
A tiny house built during mission times.
One of thirty apartments thought to be
Built by indigenous workers for their families.

19

For 150 years they've left,
Commuters traveling, bound for SF.
The on-site museum can surely be
A place to learn about rail history.

20

While burgers and burritos are okay,
The best part about this small cafe:
The photo-loving owner who, for some fun,
Will add your pic to his massive collection.

Alviso

Back before highways or even rail lines connected San Jose to San Francisco and the rest of the world, the small Port of Alviso on the marshy southern tip of the San Francisco Bay was the main shipping and transportation hub for travel to and from San Jose. Alviso was annexed by San Jose in 1968, so this rural-feeling community is technically part of the city. This hunt stretches from areas of Santa Clara north of Highway 101, up into the historic core of Alviso.

1

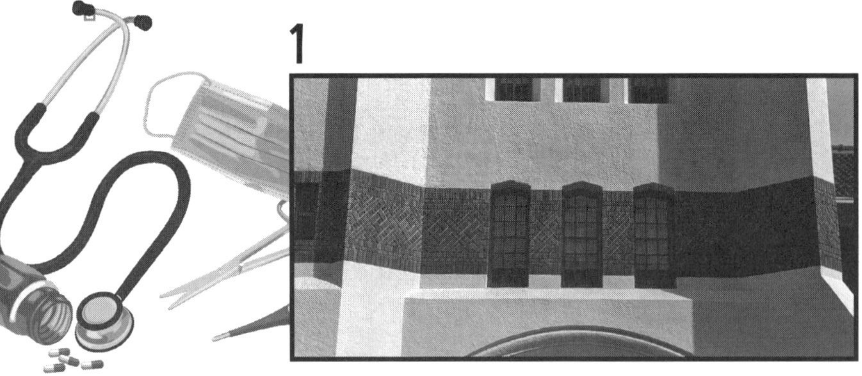

The site of our county's greatest tragedy,
More than one hundred lives lost, none could flee.
This rebuilt tower is all that remains;
Today a tech company holds the reins.

2

A round brick building dates to days long past,
Cloaked by a modern apartment complex.
Built by a wealthy man to win a lost love,
Look down toward it from the trail above.

3

A site that's unique in Santa Clara,
The last untouched land in the area.
The name comes from an Ohlone locution,
Meaning "the place where baskets are woven."

4

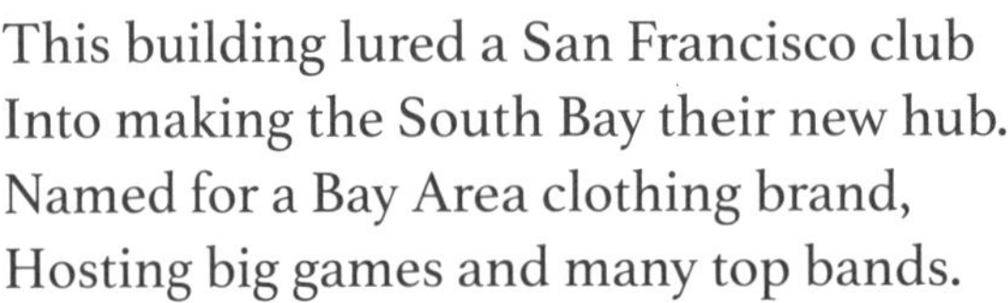

This building lured a San Francisco club
Into making the South Bay their new hub.
Named for a Bay Area clothing brand,
Hosting big games and many top bands.

5

Protesting in 1973
Poor public services and local poverty.
Activists built a "toll plaza" to collect
Funds from everyone who hoped to transect.

6

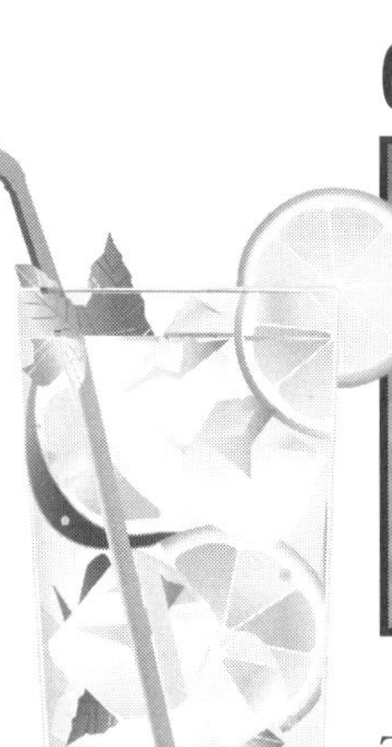

The most-loved restaurant and bar in town
Transports you back to an era long gone.
Comfort food and drink to close out the day,
A place to gather, where locals will stay.

7

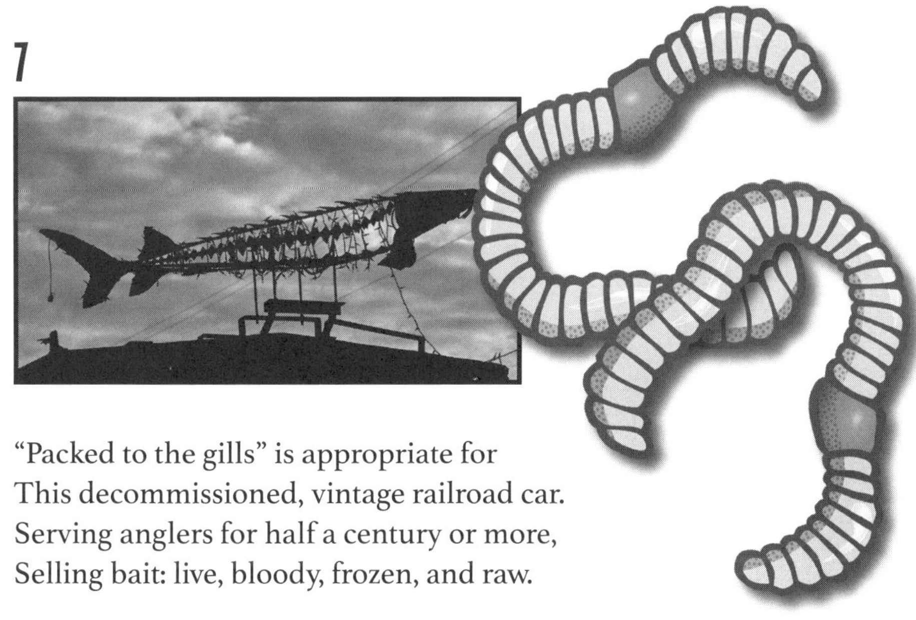

"Packed to the gills" is appropriate for
This decommissioned, vintage railroad car.
Serving anglers for half a century or more,
Selling bait: live, bloody, frozen, and raw.

8

Standing all alone, the last of this kind,
One of many Victorians, most lost to time.
This historic home, now restored to last,
A hint of the town's once-booming past.

9

At one time, this vacant building would rate
The third-largest cannery in the States.
Signs the owner here was so renowned:
the largest funeral in SF Chinatown.

10

When the town was a major shipping port,
This building held goods before they went out.
With massive walls inside, at eight feet thick,
Foods were kept cool by these layers of brick.

11

Definitely a place that time forgot,
Whether you have a boat or a yacht,
Dating back to when this port was a path,
Shipping by water to SF and Sac.

Critical habitat in the South Bay,
Coming to life after years of decay.
This waterfront park is the place to stalk
Birds, sunsets, and photogenic boardwalks.

Milpitas

Milpitas means roughly "little cornfields" in Spanish, and for most of its history was a rural farming town in the valley between the Bay and the Diablo Hills. Today the city has a large Asian and Pacific Islander population, with significant Filipino, Indian, and Chinese communities. This hunt spans the flatland area of Milpitas.

1

When he was granted land by the Spanish gov,
Anza Party soldier didn't need a shove.
He built his home, one story of adobe,
It still stands, protected for eternity.

2

A bustling place to take a walk or play,
Look for this goalie with his legs all splayed.
Sunset on the hills is one of the perks;
On the Fourth they often shoot fireworks.

3

This vintage farmhouse at more than 175 years late,
The oldest occupied adobe in the state.
One more thing that you probably should know,
It's not in Alviso, as the name might show.

4

Come inside this suburban shopping mall,
For groceries and more, find all you can haul.
A place that could be essentially crowned
As our local Filipinotown.

5

Joyful leap as if (finally!) they've found
A new home for which they are eagerly bound.
Stop in here to see opportunities,
To make a new friend for your family.

6

This place to play or to get fit beckons,
Or to learn about ancient traditions.
Enroll in a South Asian language course,
Take yoga from someone who learned at the source.

7

Looks like school's out and they've been freed,
Where generations of kids have studied.
Even today you can go here to learn
From a computer or from pages that turn.

8

The city's melting pot is this strip mall,
Chinese, Indian, Japanese, and all.
Outside of this major grocery chain,
Find jumping fish as if feeding they strain.

East Foothills

The Diablo Mountain Range, known locally as the Diablo Hills or East Foothills, marks the eastern boundary of Santa Clara County. This hunt stretches from points in the Diablo Hills just east of Milpitas, through miles of unincorporated county land, and then south through the hills into San Jose's Evergreen and Silver Creek neighborhoods. It would be challenging to cover this vast, hilly route without a car.

1

High above the land, they rise like a spine,
Possibly built for cattle, sheep, or swine?
By whom they were erected, when and why,
Is unknown, and the stories multiply.

2

Where a one-room schoolhouse today still stands,
Once it educated children of ranch hands.
A windy stretch on Calaveras Road,
Later a barn, now where stuff is stored.

3

Conventional, organic, and free-range,
White, brown, and types you might think strange.
This farm market sells a variety,
Even a budget sort, "checked and dirty."

4

Every spring we are all given this gift,
The chance to gaze at a sight that uplifts.
A private garden with thousands of blooms
In every color, and unique heirlooms.

____

____

5

Cattle and oak trees and burrowing owls,
Dense fog in the morning, now a coyote yowls.
Offering the chance to flee the hustle,
Epic sunsets and a route named kestrel.

____

____

6

Once upon a time, a sweltering bath
Drew people from all over to this path.
The mineral waters were said to heal
Nearly any ailment that you might feel.

7

The sound of haunting chants, where vows are said,
And only the most devoted do tread.
They give their lives to serve with their brethen
They'll leave on you a lasting impression.

8

Seeking acclaim for all eternity,
A rich man gave a gift for all to see.
A portal to explore was his bequest,
And, for himself, a final place to rest.

9

A holy place to gather, study, pray,
And plan for seva, service is their forte.
There's a grand kitchen where veggie food
Is shared and free to all, in gratitude.

10

Huddled together under the night sky,
With kindly professors as expert guides.
A rare look into the heavens above,
Nearest spot to space, what all kids dream of.

11

Experiments in flight, risks he withstood,
A winged contraption he named for the 'hood.
One last day, the professor met his match
On his final flight, a break he couldn't catch.

12

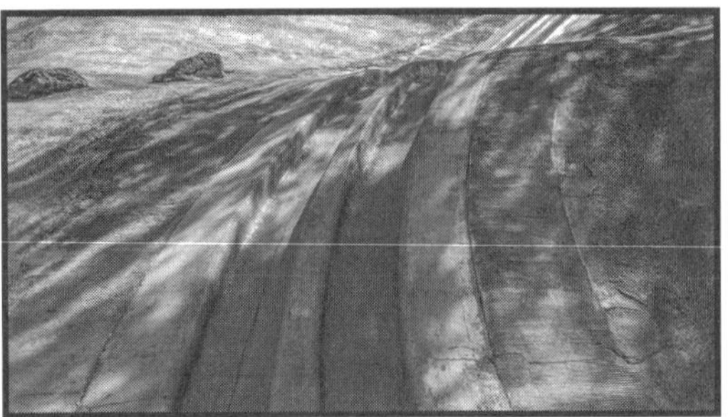

Down a cement channel this curving run,
Where kids of all ages have retro fun.
Be sure to bring a box or you will find
Serious risk of burning your behind.

Campbell

In 1888, Benjamin Campbell split off part of the land he owned for the creation of a new town around the railroad stop. This primarily agricultural community came to be known as the Orchard City, a nickname still used today. This hunt stretches from points in and around downtown Campbell, then heads north on Winchester Boulevard into West San Jose.

1

Far away from the Mighty Mississip,
Find this boat docked near the Los Gatos Creek.
While you are doing this regular chore,
Hand-feed koi or browse the quirky gift store.

2

There's no telling what treasures you'll find
While poking around this wacky gold mine.
Unique furniture, decor, jewelry,
Collectibles, even taxidermy.

3

It's definitely not the quality
Bringing folks to this storied eatery.
A place to score late-night grub for cheap:
On weekends they're open until three.

4

Historic scenes and a tribute,
Growing, packing, and canning fruit.
Picking apricots at their peak,
Find this one up above the creek.

5

Originally built on Hamilton,
Later moved to be about one mile on.
This quaint Cotswold cottage was perfect for
An English-born, local fruit pioneer.

6

Standing on the corner this brick building,
Among the oldest, first built for banking.
Dating back to the eighteen nineties,
Serving workers at local canneries.

7

Campbell's oldest public structure,
Fighting fires is what it was built for.
The town uses it currently
To share stories of history.

8

Providing one crucial supply
That helped the Orchard City grow.
You can see it from far and wide,
Something that all local folks know.

9

This land once held by the town's founder.
He gave it to his son, who built a house here.
At this ornate, Queen Anne-style, cottage abode,
The couple made butter and cream to be sold.

10

Don't get on the wrong side of
This fierce vintage mascot.
He promotes their tech's training,
And keeps watch over the shop.

____

____

11

This local restaurant serves up a ton
Of comforting foods like lemon chicken.
Only open since 1985,
Their sign dates to a mid-century time.

____

____

12

Built back in 1938
And funded by the WPA,
This former school site is where
Local performing arts are shared.

13

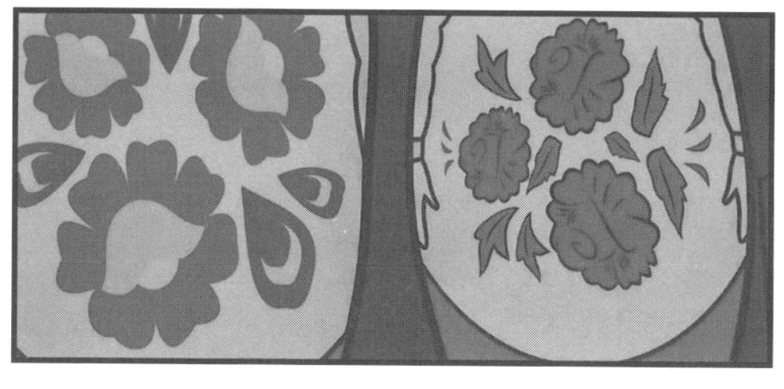

Where this vast selection always includes,
East European and North Asian groceries.
Stop in here for an assortment of foods:
Borscht, pickles, caviar, and pirozkis.

14

This grocery serves their community
Selling bulk food in unlabeled baggies.
Spices, grains, green coffee, and legumes,
Typical, hard-to-source, Ethiopian foods.

15

It started as a simple farmhouse home,
Before a momentous transformation.
Now 160 plus rooms to roam,
What an unusual renovation!

16

Though once joined by two other twins,
This retro spot now stands alone.
Called a historic protection win,
Though its future is still unknown.

Los Gatos

This town at the base of the Santa Cruz mountains was named "La Rinconada de Los Gatos" (cat's corner) because the early settlers could hear mountain lions calling at night. Today the town has popular regional parks and a busy downtown business district. This hunt stretches from north to south through the town of Los Gatos.

1

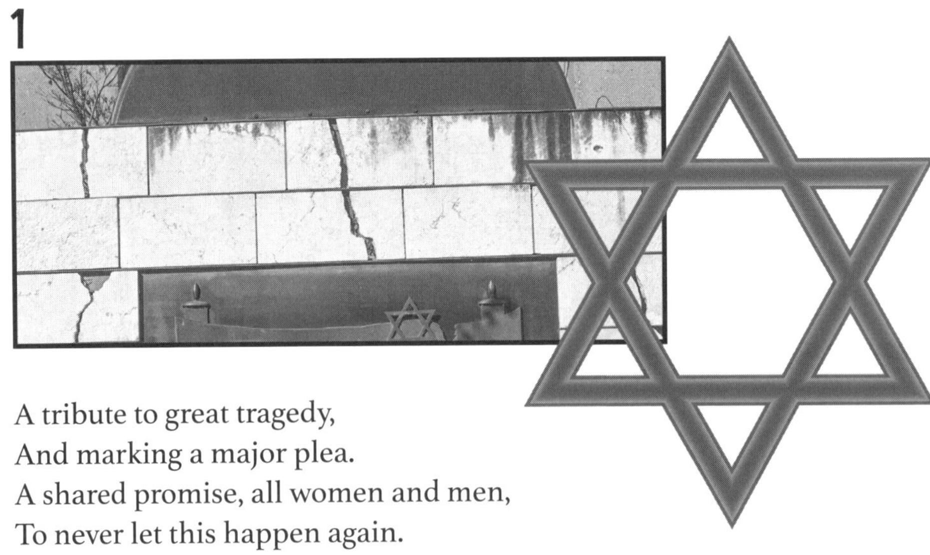

A tribute to great tragedy,
And marking a major plea.
A shared promise, all women and men,
To never let this happen again.

2

Outside the global headquarters
Of a now well-recognized name.
Used by many when looking for
Something new to binge, not the same.

3

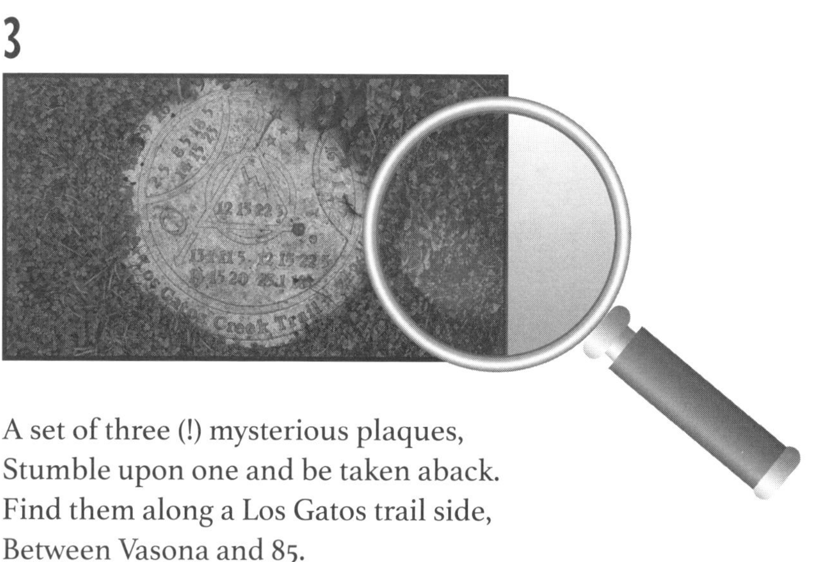

A set of three (!) mysterious plaques,
Stumble upon one and be taken aback.
Find them along a Los Gatos trail side,
Between Vasona and 85.

4

Storing this essential resource,
while guarding our local supply.
And providing great space of course,
For a dog walk, hike, or bike ride.

5

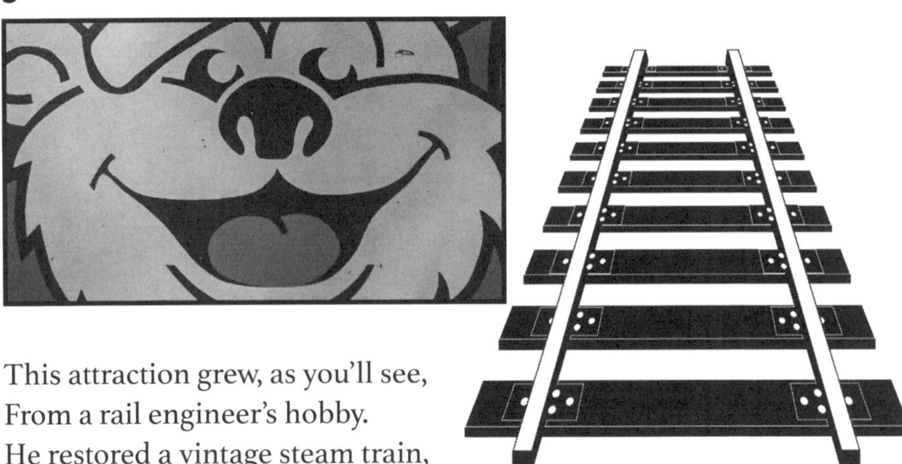

This attraction grew, as you'll see,
From a rail engineer's hobby.
He restored a vintage steam train,
And let kids ride for free back then.

Before the Canal, built in the UK
Then shipped around the Horn to the Bay.
Later part of a traveling circus,
Constantly rotating, it is endless!

7

A unique place for groups to meet
And get Italian food to eat,
While playing a lesser-known game
On a court that's gotten acclaim.

8

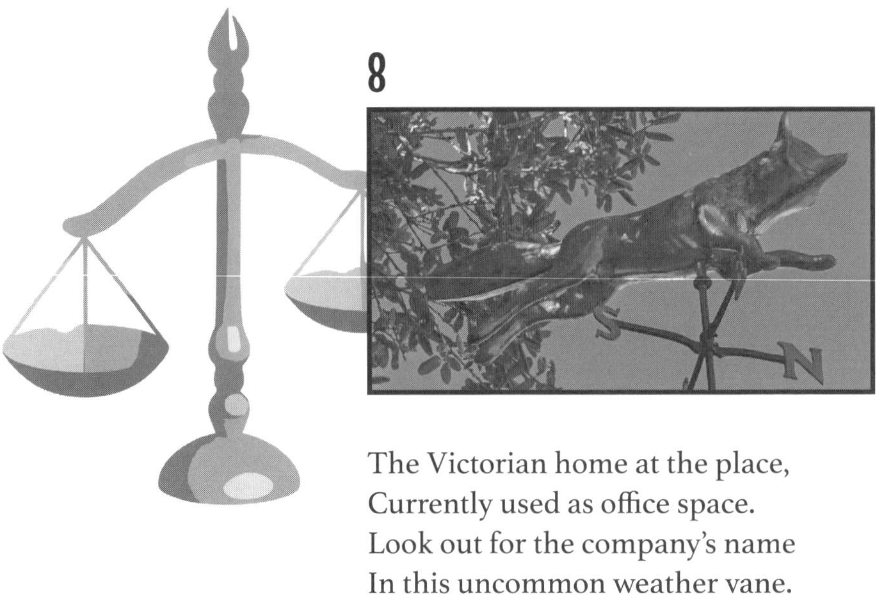

The Victorian home at the place,
Currently used as office space.
Look out for the company's name
In this uncommon weather vane.

9

This Victorian, surrounded by palm trees,
A mortuary for years, more than 50.
Now a restaurant serving Island fare,
Said to be haunted, with ghosts spotted there.

10

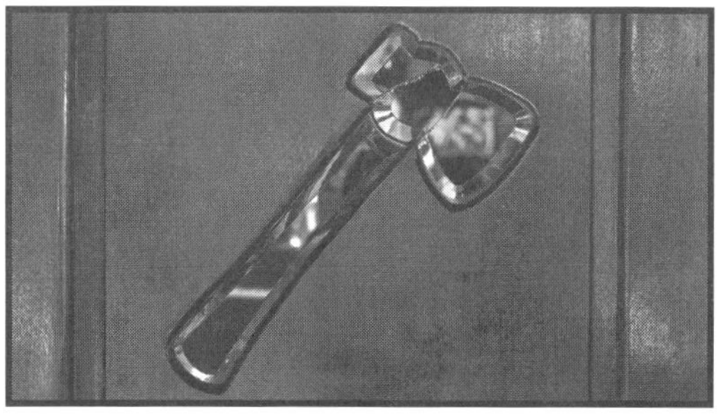

Named for an odd figure in history,
A temperance activist and zealot.
Known for traveling around the country
And destroying taverns with her hatchet.

11

This structure with a witch hat canopy,
A town icon and an enduring site.
The building's name is Spanish for "valley,"
Recallling the Valley of Heart's Delight.

12

This independently run downtown store,
Carrying supplies for home, farm, and more.
It's been there for years since this town was rural
Still today, stocking mountain essentials.

13

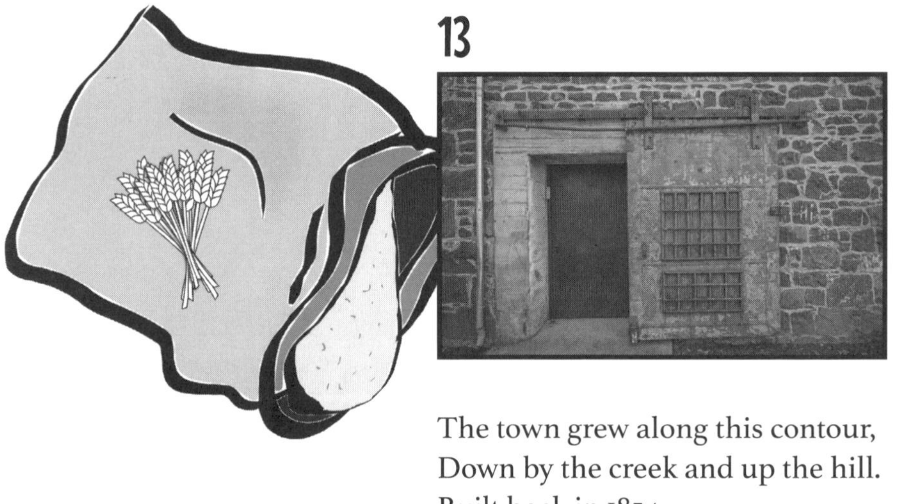

The town grew along this contour,
Down by the creek and up the hill.
Built back in 1854,
Was this four-story, stone flour mill.

14

In front of an organization
Known for historic preservation.
Find this flame burning outside,
Honoring service and sacrifice.

15

The words on this old wooden post,
In Chinese mean "radiant light."
For some time, this supportive host
Helped young girls that others would slight.

16

Guarding the entry to a closed estate,
These felines stand watch beside the gate.
"Leo" and "Leona," these animals here,
Have guarded this site for one hundred years.

Saratoga

This community at the base of the Santa Cruz Mountains grew up around a sawmill and a toll road, built to transport lumber in 1850. There was once a natural mineral spring here that had similar chemical content to the waters at, namesake, Saratoga Springs, New York. In the twentieth century, this agricultural community drew visitors from all over to the annual Blossom Festival. This hunt stretches from downtown Saratoga into the adjacent hills.

1

Outside of a dog, a book is man's best friend.
Inside of a dog, it's too dark to read.

Next to an orchard from a time long past,
A place free for all to learn things that last.
The side patio shares some wit and wisdom,
then go inside to pick out something fun.

2

Renowned architect in 1915
Designed the interiors, redwood pristine.
"Dark wood, rose window," for westerly light
Creates a "distinctive look," she would write.

3

Year after year marked on a redwood slab,
Sharing points in time and memories we have.
Next to a tribute, the last sacrifice,
Local war heroes who gave all: their life.

4

Local people raised funds to build
A place where readers would be thrilled.
Today it's a different "why,"
Not to borrow, only to buy.

5

One of the oldest homes standing in town,
In the 1860s, roots were put down,
Built by one blacksmith, sold to another,
The local mountain redwood's a feature.

6

Sheltering passengers from wind and rain,
Back before cars were easy to attain.
First standing nearby a Japanese inn,
Connecting the South Bay, the interurban.

7

Mister McCarty used to levy a fare,
All who passed his tollgate paid their share.
Look for the historic marker right here,
Sharing past names: Tollgate and McCartysville.

8

Before the railroad, this foothill town
was cut off from other enclaves around.
Horse-drawn coaches ran from here and carried
passengers to other communities.

9

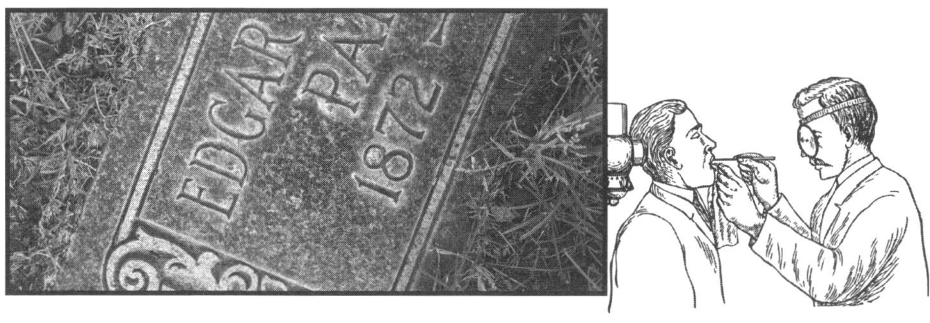

One odd local dentist made a great fuss
And wore teeth he'd strung up on a necklace.
In a marketing move, he changed his name
From Edgar to "Painless," as he'd exclaim.

10

Designed to be a holiday retreat,
Long-traveled artisans designed this feat.
Today folks come to wander this garden,
and, in the spring, see cherry blossoms.

11

Built at first to harvest lime from the earth,
Now access to nature brings its highest worth.
Find modern trails for those wishing to flee,
Hike it from Saratoga to the sea.

12

A palace of art, now a public park,
Built for a senator, now a landmark.
And named for the guy who penned one grand dame,
Queen Calafia, our state's namesake.

Cupertino

Early pioneer settler Elisha Stephens (also spelled "Stevens"), captain of the first wagon train to cross the Sierra Nevada, settled in what is now called Cupertino. Other early residents planted vineyards along Montebello Ridge, and later, fruit orchards on the flatlands. The area stayed primarily agricultural for more than 100 years. Today the majority of Cupertino's population identifies as Asian, with large Chinese and Indian communities. This hunt stretches across the city.

1

In a sprawling olive grove, you'll see,
A brand inspired by another fruit tree.
The name evokes a museum or more,
But really it's just a company store.

2

A rural schoolhouse has stood on this land
Since a few years past the Civil War's end.
Remodeled back in the Craftsman era,
With period shingles and new bell tower.

3

Since '48 they've been family-owned,
Full of ideas for greening your home.
For inside and out, whatever you dream,
And expert advice from their design team.

4

Built as a weekend home for a rich guy,
Modeled on the palace of Versailles.
Once facing demolition, it survived
And moved here to be a history archive.

5

Have a glimpse into far-off galaxies,
And live out your space travel fantasies.
Open to all with tickets for sale,
Check out what the performance will unveil.

6

In the year 1776,
Anza's party camped here, then in the sticks.
On the banks of the nearby Stevens Creek,
Marked today where kids and their parents meet.

7

The old ranch of a local pioneer,
For whom the creek it bisects is named for.
Honored for being the captain of the
First wagon train to cross the Sierra.

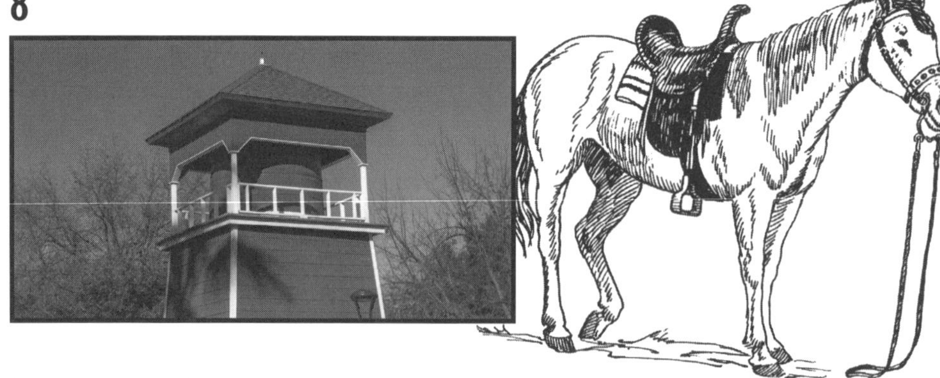

In the '30s and '40s this site served
As a horse ranch, now forever preserved.
This birding hot spot hosts the office of
The South Bay's leading avian club.

Sunnyvale

In 1841, Martin Murphy, Jr., one of the earliest pioneer settlers to come overland to the Santa Clara Valley, acquired land and set up a farm in a town they then called Murphy. Later renamed Sunnyvale, the community was mostly agricultural until after the 1906 earthquake when town promoters convinced Hendy Iron Works to relocate from San Francisco. Other businesses followed, and today the city is home to a mix of industry, tech campuses, and residential neighborhoods. This hunt stretches across the city.

1

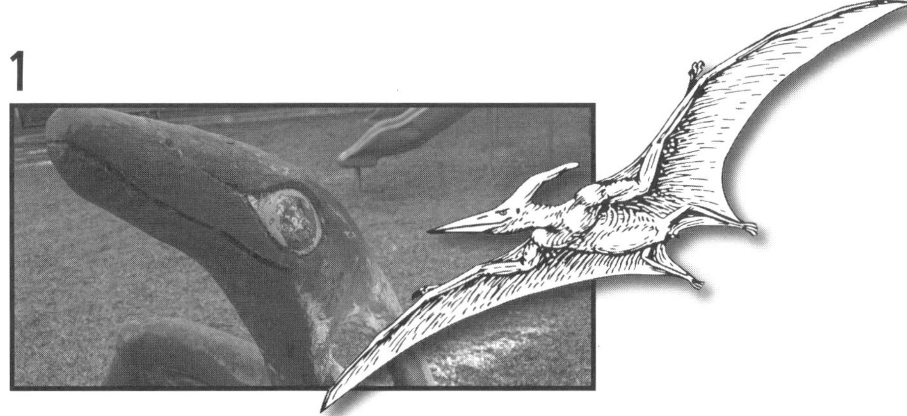

Since the sixties little kids would meet
To play among these prehistoric beasts.
On the hunt for these quirky dinosaurs,
there are a lot of local parks to explore!

2

Before this was a suburban household,
They produced wine and brandy to be sold.
From a private rail on this property,
They shipped 300 gallons of wine daily.

3

Once a computer store owned by Woz's bro,
Both he and Jobs visited as the brand would grow.
Here's the place where many locals said, "Gosh!"
At their very first Apple or Macintosh.

4

This redwood farmhouse, the oldest around
Built with a Civil War background.
Made for an East Coast miner turned farmer,
The tank out front is what it's known for.

5

Honoring our local ag legacy,
The city preserved these apricot trees.
Learn about locals who toiled day and night
To build the Valley of the Heart's Delight.

6

As the old Murphy house was left to decay,
They bulldozed it to build the expressway.
Rebuilt years later, this reproduction,
works to promote local preservation.

7

In the not-too-distant past, this was where
You could buy fruit and seasonal fare.
Founders of, they were jokingly said to be,
Sunnyvale State University.

Pass this guy quick and do a double take,
Showing the best way to spend your lunch break.
Deeply engrossed in a book, at his knee,
You'll find he has twins in seven other cities.

9

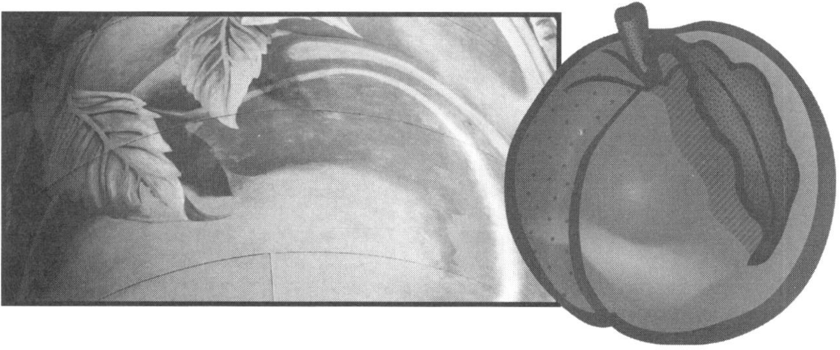

On this site, back in the nineteen twenties,
One of the largest canning factories.
This curious tower up in the air,
Once supplied water to the whole square.

10

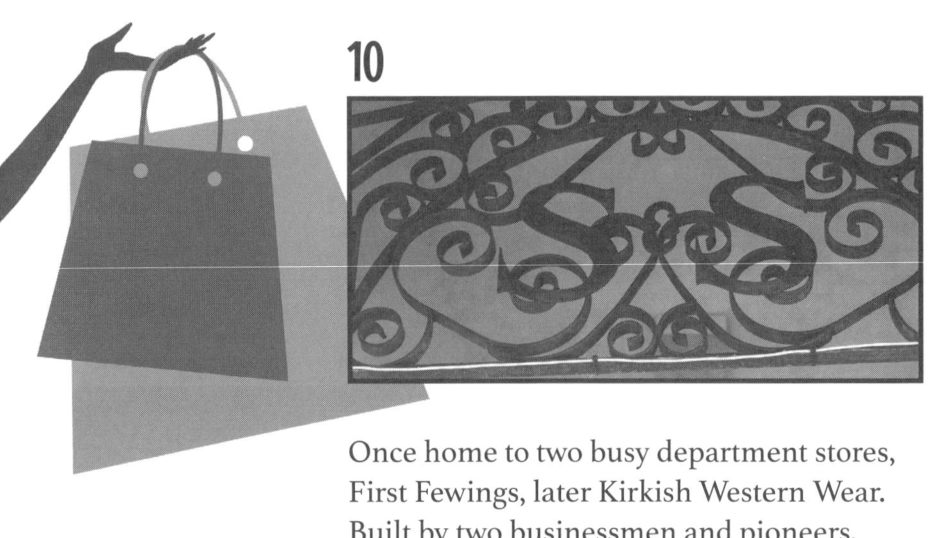

Once home to two busy department stores,
First Fewings, later Kirkish Western Wear.
Built by two businessmen and pioneers,
Both called Charles, find their initials here.

11

Despite shifting interests over the years,
This has always been an entertainment hub.
First cinema, later adult film reels,
Most recently as a booming nightclub.

12

Once, a popular bakery,
Owned by a Spanish family.
Named for the depot across the street,
Today it's where readers like to meet.

13

This was once part of a large cannery
For a successful national fruit brand.
Later for a seed laboratory,
Moved across the street where it now stands.

14

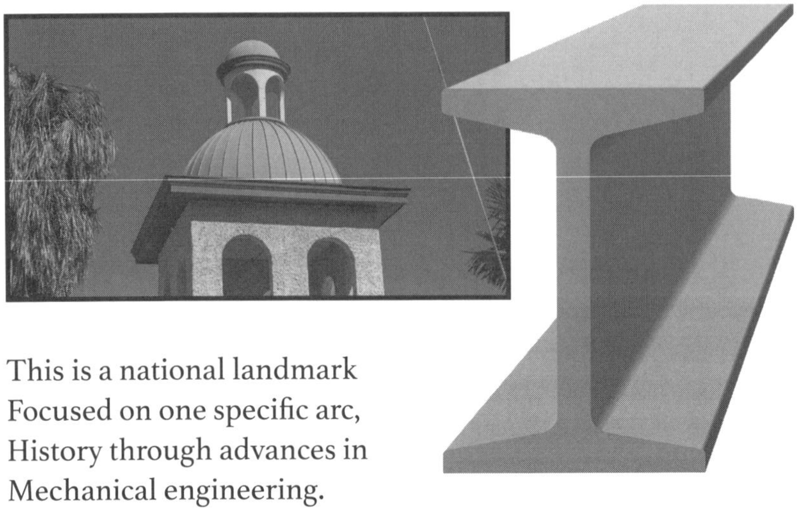

This is a national landmark
Focused on one specific arc,
History through advances in
Mechanical engineering.

15

In a typical cul-de-sac
Right in the middle of the path,
You'll see this antique street lamp
Built at the nearby iron plant.

Los Altos

This small downtown of Los Altos grew up after 1907, when a train station was built to move local agricultural products through the region. Later, local farms were subdivided and it was promoted as a primarily residential community, as it remains today. This hunt stretches across the city.

1

The legend says that this ranch house is where
Two young tech founders built their first hardware.
Though Woz himself said that this is just wrong,
Selfie-seeking tourists stop by in throngs.

2

A lovely house under a large oak tree,
Despite one famed owner, there's no mystery.
Later sold off to a wealthy tycoon,
Leading to the railroad and new downtown.

3

A home built for the town's founder,
On land from a, now famous, neighbor.
President of the SP railroad,
And a member of Stanford's board.

4

When the railroad first roared into town,
Here's where passengers came to board.
Today, a fancy coffee shop,
Look out for the caboose backdrop.

5

A magical place for kids young and old,
To come and discover a brand new world.
Between the pages or through something new,
Games, toys, crafts, and things for grown-ups, too.

6

A portal to different days and times,
This example of photorealism shines.
Sharing local history through photos,
Objects, and memories that time has froze.

7

This rustic and shingled, Craftsman-style farmhouse
Is typical of early orchard homes.
This one was donated to the city,
And now it hosts local art and history.

8

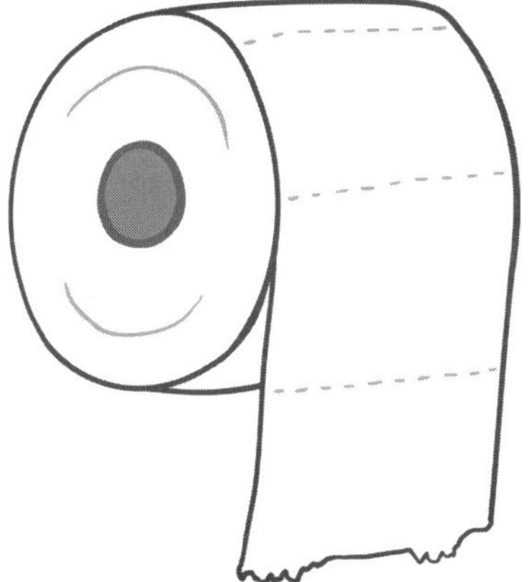

This once common place to relieve your bladder,
Moved from a ranch that once stood on Grant Road.
With the same last name as this book's author:
It's funny to see your name on a commode!

Mountain View

The town of Mountain View started off as a stagecoach stop between San Francisco and San Jose. Named for the community's broad views of the Santa Cruz Mountains, the city has played an important role in the development of Silicon Valley. Pioneering technology companies were founded here, and still today Mountain View hosts major corporate headquarters, most notably, Google. This hunt stretches across the city from the downtown core to the Bay.

1

Oldest commercial building in the county,
First a general store on Castro Street.
Founded by brothers with a German name,
Now it's home to a local sandwich chain.

2

This sturdy building was the town's first bank,
Though the windows were once blown out in a prank.
First Farmers and Merchants, later B of A,
Now a storied place in the tech community.

3

For more than ten years it caused many to frown,
Towering unfinished over downtown.
Nicknamed "Free Dog City" or the "Dog Pound,"
For the pack of guard dogs roaming the grounds.

4

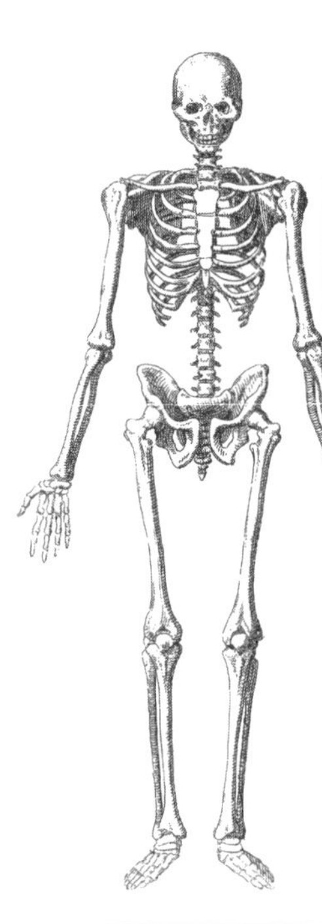

Secrets are hidden in these rolling hills,
A bustling park, once a site of burials.
Some bodies were moved, though some still remain,
Resting under the fields and kids at play.

5

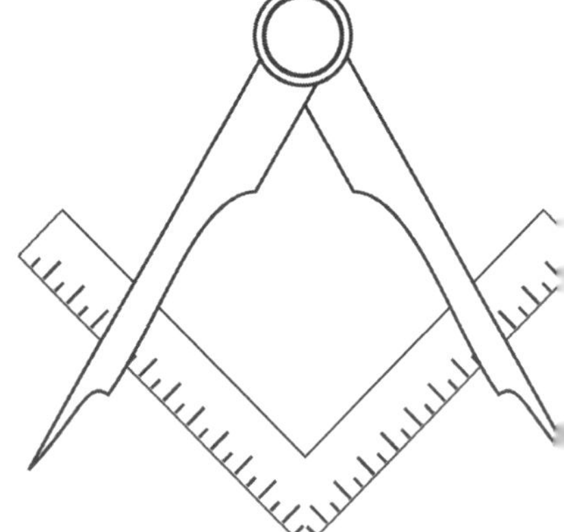

Now home to a fraternal club,
Members gather and have some grub.
First built as a veterans hall,
Find this flag on the highest wall.

6

Where old Mountain View High used to be,
There's a rental community.
Watch for these old school front reliefs
On the side facing Castro Street.

7

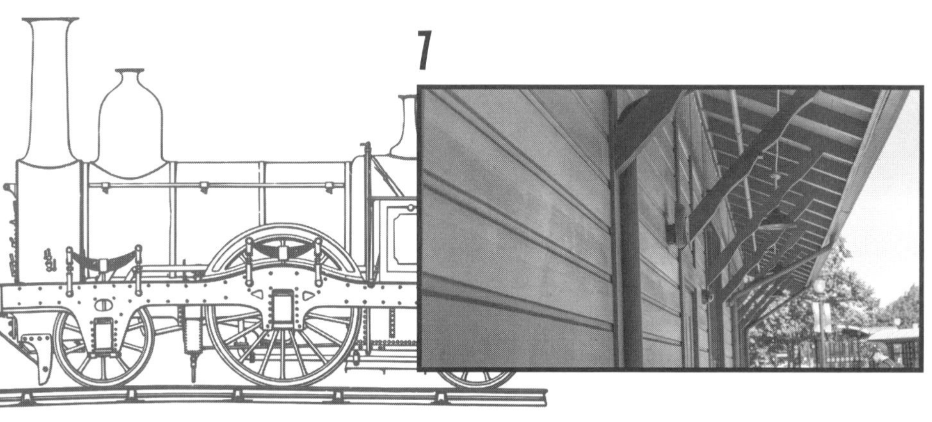

First built in 1888,
For the Southern Pacific rail.
Though it looks old, it replicates
The original, true to scale.

8

I'm sure that you know downtown as Castro,
But it was initially one mile fro.
A stage stop on a, then rural, pathway,
Now, where El Camino meets a freeway.

9

Where families gather to celebrate,
and keep their village traditions in spate.
Look up to this iconic royal crown
symbol of the festa for which the site's named.

Where can you go to see technology,
The earliest in written history?
This museum starts by sharing that fare,
Then shows you to more modern hardware.

11

This lovely home and vintage water tank,
Carefully restored, the city we thank.
One of the first homes built in Mountain View,
All around it the community grew.

Palo Alto

The town of Palo Alto was incorporated in 1894 to serve the newly founded Stanford University. The tree-lined downtown business district along University Avenue is popular for shopping, food, and entertainment. This hunt covers addresses in the City of Palo Alto (excluding Stanford), starting from the downtown core to Mountain View, and then toward Los Altos Hills.

1

Soaring above San Francisquito Creek,
The community's elder namesake.
1769 was the year
When explorer Portola's team camped here.

2

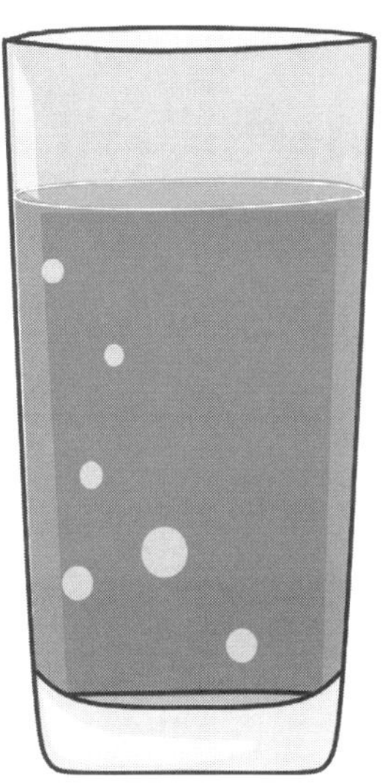

Always a home for new technology,
A first to build this sort of utility.
A reinforced tank sized to never go dry,
Closed, once we tapped into the state supply.

3

The first office of a famed company,
Back when their brand name was prefaced by "The."
Find this address right off downtown's main street,
Bearing this unusual nameplate.

Dating to the earliest film era,
Once called the "Pride of the Peninsula."
Carefully restored, thanks to a tech heir,
Now featuring classic Hollywood fare.

5

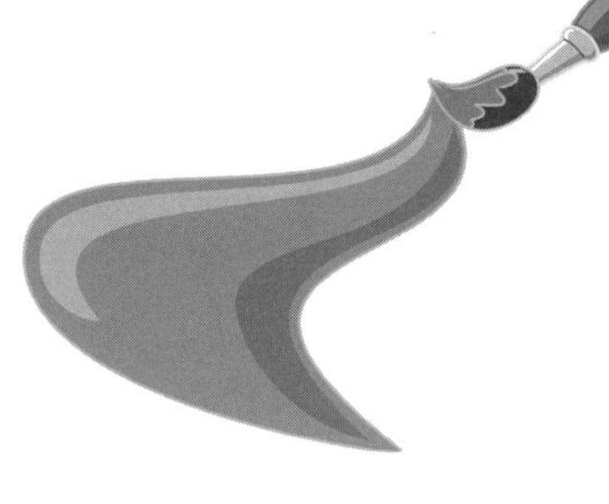

A local artist known for trompe-l'oeil,
Illusions that, in French, mean "fool the eye."
Hidden through town, I hope you'll explore,
This one's right beside a furniture store.

6

Another by the same artist,
This one on a federal site.
Posed and ready to cast a line.
Real or not? Look close and see if you're right.

7

This storefront on University
Was a cafe known in music history.
Legends performed at open mic, it's said,
With names like Jerry Garcia and Joan Baez.

Designed by esteemed architect named Weeks,
To draw more shoppers to Hamilton Street.
The pilasters have a unique appeal,
Oddly inspired by the automobile.

9

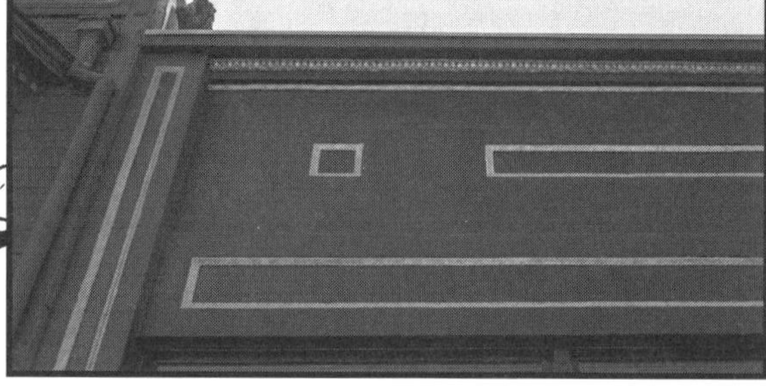

Since opening in the nineteen thirties,
stocked floor to ceiling, each nook and cranny.
Offering tomes, new, rare, and classics,
To curious locals and academics.

A grand home first owned by a descendent
And namesake of a US president.
This early Stanford Classics professor
Made a hobby of predicting the weather.

11

This average house might surprise you to be
Called the "birthplace of Silicon Valley."
On this site, two accomplished founders made
Products that changed our lives in many ways.

12

Hidden below these towering redwoods,
This museum exhibits unique goods.
Everyday technology and machines,
Innovations from the last century.

____

____

13

This bungalow on an aptly-named street
Hosted a bit of music history.
Where, while influenced by a psych substance,
They chose a name now held with reverence.

____

____

14

A place to explore the tranquility
Of gardens cared for meticulously.
Owned by a woman for eight decades,
Then given to the city for public space.

15

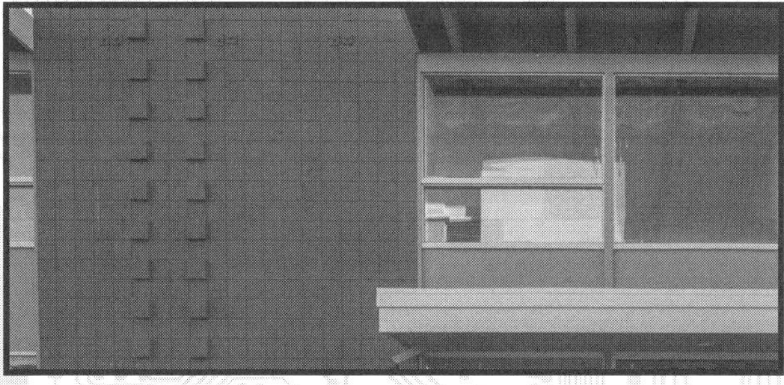

Once the office of a tech pioneer
Who helped to bring our digital world near.
The essential product they helped equip,
A tiny, silicon-based microchip.

16

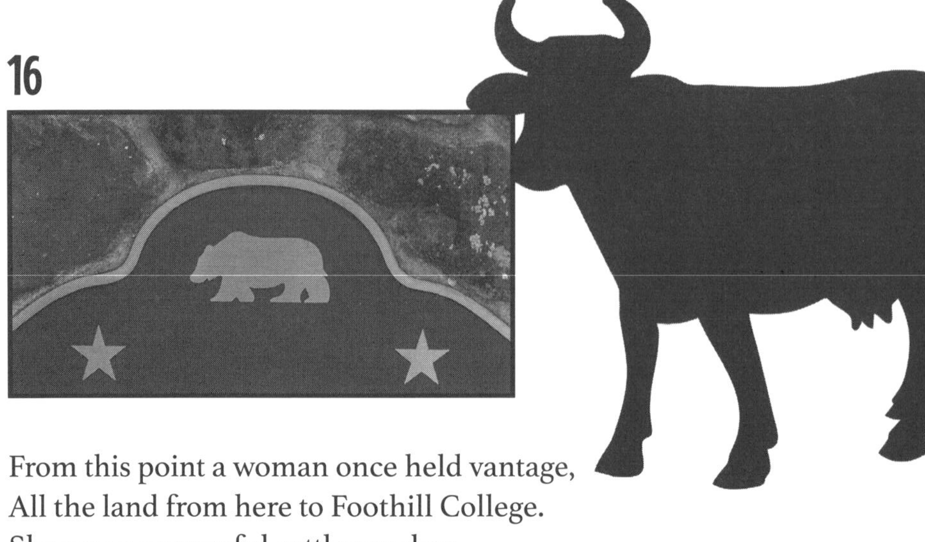

From this point a woman once held vantage,
All the land from here to Foothill College.
She was a successful cattle rancher,
Business woman, and a caring healer.

Stanford

Railroad baron Leland Stanford and his wife, Jane Lathrop Stanford, founded Stanford University in 1876, endowing it with thousands of acres of land. Today this renowned university is the largest college campus in the United States, featuring interesting landmarks, architecture, and art warranting a dedicated route. This hunt covers sites on the Stanford University campus and in the surrounding residential neighborhoods. Be sure to park in a dedicated visitor parking lot, take public transit, or ride a bike.

1

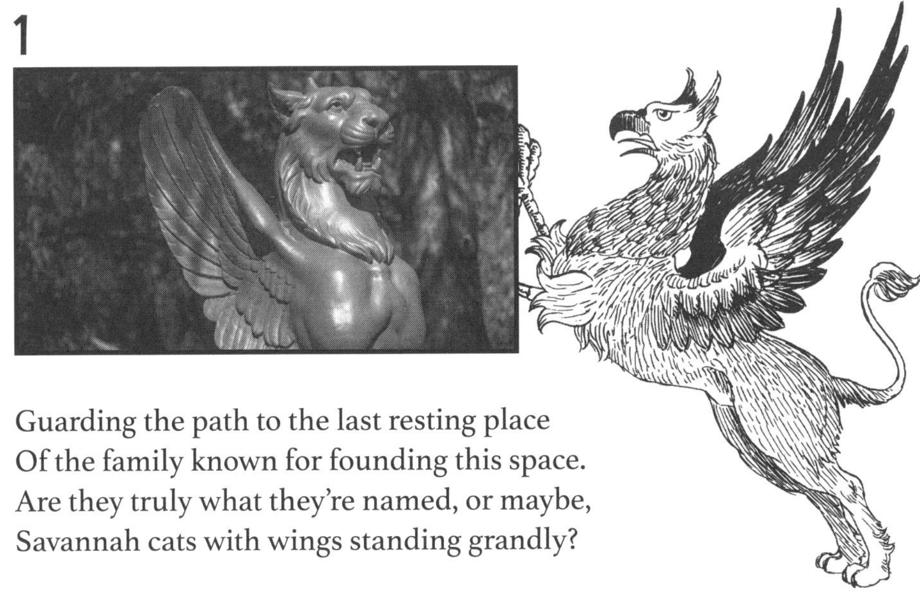

Guarding the path to the last resting place
Of the family known for founding this space.
Are they truly what they're named, or maybe,
Savannah cats with wings standing grandly?

2

Built to mark loss and a parent's worst fear,
Everything is a memorial here.
But this specific spot is meant to be
Where to go to honor this family.

3

Crafted to honor Jane's brother at rest,
Who lived with her after her husband passed.
Modeled on a famous statue in Rome,
Her brother was buried beneath this stone.

4

Planned for the Stanfords in the early days,
Ones that thrive in the summer's hottest rays.
It is always a stunning place to be,
Standing in the shadow of a Joshua tree.

5

Working on these figures for many years,
Sadly, dying before his plan was clear.
Others stepped in to mount it as he might,
But no one can be sure they did it right.

6

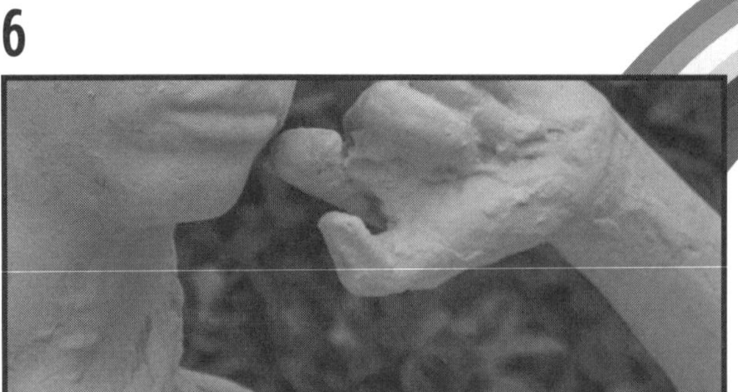

Built to honor the Stonewall uprising,
And urge love instead of despising.
Two seated women and two standing men,
The tribute has a twin in Manhattan.

7

While the whole campus was built for her son,
Jane built this one place for her lost husband.
One of the first open like this in the West,
This gathering place seats 1,200 guests.

8

At almost three hundred feet tall,
Looking over the campus mall,
This structure hosts one top-ranked,
Conservative-leaning think tank.

9

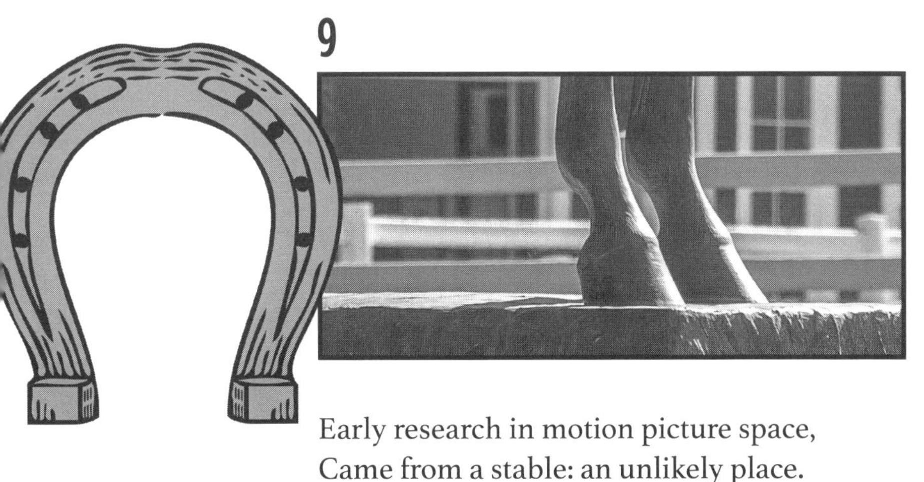

Early research in motion picture space,
Came from a stable: an unlikely place.
Tests proved Stanford's theory that when a mare
Trots, for a moment, all legs are in the air.

10

When the Great Quake took down the church belfry,
They saved and moved the old clock, you see.
Still wound by hand twice every single week,
This antique gem is worth taking a peek.

11

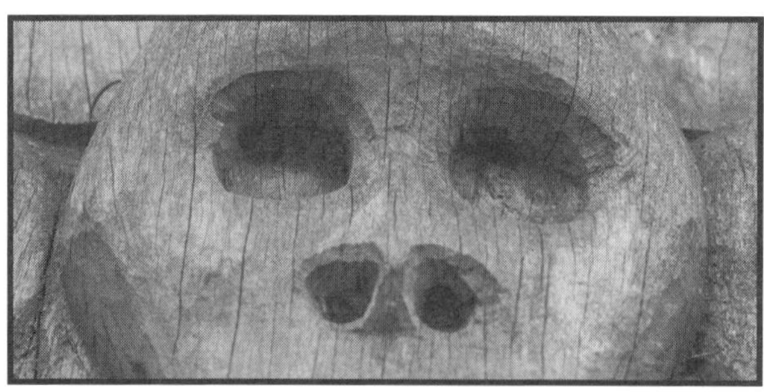

Look up into this shaded canopy,
At unique South Pacific artistry.
The towering creations found in this park,
Share mythical figures carved into bark.

12

A simple plaque near the scene of a crime
Shares powerful words that stirred hearts and minds.
"You took away my worth," she started to say,
"My safety," "my own voice," " . . . until today."

13

On San Juan Hill, overlooking campus,
Is a house whose most famous tenant was
A US president and his family
Who moved back here in the nineteen thirties.

Designed for a professor's family,
Based on an unusual geometry.
Collected spaces shaped like hexagons;
No right angles in the floor plan were drawn.

15

This school-owned, scientific contraption
Is still used to collect information.
Centered on an expansive open space,
The trails nearby are a popular place.

16

It's not very common in our nation
To spot a medieval fortification.
This unique structure on a winding road,
Along where the Matadero Creek flows.

Morgan Hill

This agricultural community started off as a railroad stop, then called Huntington, near the country estate owned by Diana and Hiram Morgan Hill. When the town incorporated in 1906, they changed the name, in part because of the visitors who asked for the train to stop at "Morgan Hill's ranch." While the town is still rooted in agriculture, it's a growing residential community. This hunt stretches across the city.

1

This broad vista point is where you can see
The mostly undeveloped Coyote Valley.
You'll pass bay and oak trees on this loop walk,
Winter creeks, and outcrops of our state rock.

2

First standing at Monterey and East Dunne,
Split into pieces and moved, one by one.
An ambitious work of preservation,
Now used once again for education.

3

This home of the town's namesake,
A lovely place to take a break.
Explore some local history
Amidst the rose bushes you see.

4

This place is unique for two things combined,
First, they are one of the last of their kind.
Second, dedicated to the pursuit
Of growing rare varieties of fruit.

5

Tucked within this busy strip mall
Is a place with something for all.
To laugh or to cry, with brow furled,
Or to uncover a brand new world.

6

This new, sprawling, spiritual complex,
Is certainly a photogenic spot.
Come for the chanting you are sure to hear
And wish for luck at the Lunar New Year.

7

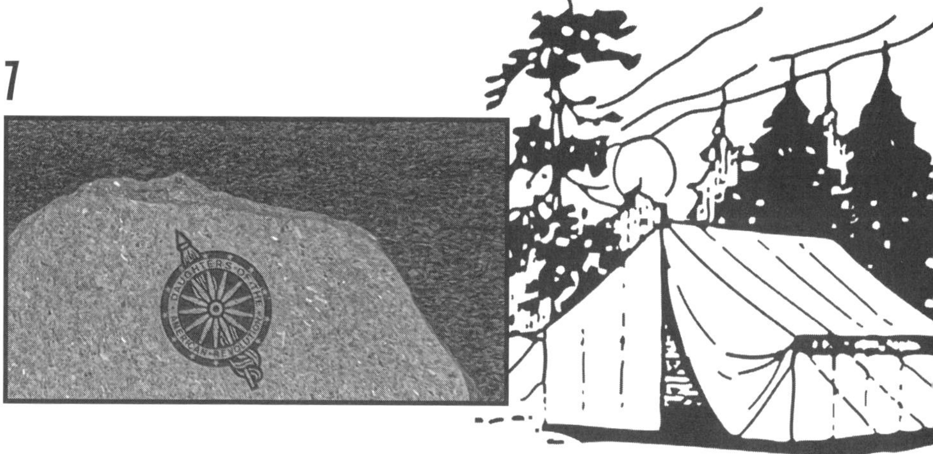

Where Anza camped after his first day,
Arriving here in the South Bay.
On Llagas Creek this marker awaits,
Take the trail west from Woodlands Estates.

8

Founded in the nineteenth century
For families in Paradise Valley.
Just about a mile from the city line,
But it feels like several steps back in time.

Gilroy

The southernmost city in Santa Clara County was incorporated in 1870. Gilroy started out as a cattle ranching and dairy hub for California. Still a largely agricultural community, the city is most famous for producing garlic and the Gilroy Garlic Festival. Today more than half of the city's residents identify as Latino. This hunt stretches across the city.

1

Funded by a wealthy Pittsburgh patron,
Equal access to books was his vision.
The city outgrew it and moved two blocks,
Now it's a museum hosting history walks.

2

Dating way back to 1855,
Built on Third, but on Fifth it now resides.
The oldest church in all the county,
Moved to appease the pastor's family.

3

Built for a couple in 1903,
Gold Rush pioneers in their family tree.
Designed by a prolific architect;
Look for this beauty in the pediment.

4

Today this old brick storefront
Is a Mexican restaurant.
Once a fire station, long ago,
Check out the dining room's fire pole!

5

Standing watch over Monterey,
High above the building's front door.
Colorful things: handmade of clay,
Pottery, tiles, and decor.

6

Built for a businessman named Wheeler,
Who got rich selling seeds to farmers.
He paid for this and the old hospital.
A member of the Elks Lodge: can you tell?

7

You've heard of the garlic, but did you know
Gilroy was once the dairy capital?
One-fifth of all butter and cheese in the state
Once came from this central creamery's freight.

8

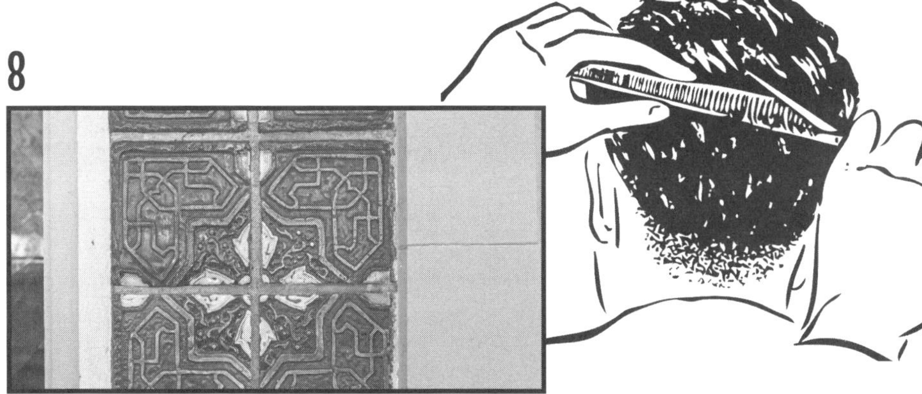

This salon and barber shop once used for
The office of an acclaimed town builder.
Today, the owner might let you look in
The vault once built to keep plans clandestine.

9

This moment, forever captured, you see,
Part of our local women's history.
Electa Ousley, the first woman in town
Granted the right to claim land on her own.

10

Since 1905 this corner building,
The "Grand Old Lady," served as many things.
City hall, courthouse, fire station, and jail,
Stop in today for a meal and an ale.

11

Local artists are working to restore
This symbol of Aztec culture and lore.
Ancient wisdom painted on this back wall.
And look up! It's more than twenty feet tall.

12

Rosy walls evoke a romantic time,
People coming from afar by this line.
Still today, South County commuters come,
For local and regional transport options.

13

First to grow garlic here commercially,
Was a guy named Jimmy Hirasaki.
Learn more about our local history
On a pathway lined by tiles like these.

14

Kids today playing handball on the court,
The evolution of an ancient sport.
A tradition, this mural salutes,
For ritual and to settle disputes.

15

Built in the '20s by architect Weeks,
Gilroy's first hospital has had some upkeep.
Still keeping our neighbors safe and healthy,
Today it's a senior community.

16

A last native speaker of Amah Mutsun tongue,
Holding community knowledge unsung.
Remembered today for this legacy,
Her name living on where learning is key.